Date of Publication
First Published 2015
Revised 2021

Copyright

Acknowledgments
I would like to thank all those who have assisted with this publication, by providing information, proof reading and all the other tasks necessary to complete it

Disclaimer
While every care has been taken in writing this publication, it is the responsibility of the reader to ensure that any action they take or propose to take complies with guidance, case law and legislation that may exist at the time. Expert legal advice may be required in respect of surveillance, nuisance and human rights issues in relation to any noise monitoring or measurements that are carried out.

Summary

This is the book that I always felt I needed when I first got involved in noise and noise measurements i.e. a simple and practical guide to some of the basics of noise and noise measurement, with pointers to more in depth information should it be needed. There are many fine text books which go into the various aspects of noise and acoustics in great detail, but that wasn't what I needed at the time. So in this book the aim is to provide some basic information on noise at an easily understood level, together with some practical advice on making noise measurements, simple calculations and interpreting reports, hopefully allowing you to avoid the most obvious errors.

I've also included some very basic information about noise nuisance, noise at work, and noise legislation that I hope will be of assistance to readers who may be less familiar with these topics.

This book is primarily focused on England & Wales, though of course the basic principles will be relevant wherever noise measurements are carried out.

This second edition was updated in 2021 to reflect changes in guidance and legislation that have occurred since the 2015 edition.

Contents

Tables

Figures

1. Introduction

Noise and Acoustics are often seen as a "black art" by many. The province of expensive consultants, acousticians and learned professors, with many complicated mathematical equations, rules and a complex and mystifying technical language. If that is how it appears to you, and yet you need or want to know some basics, (enough, for example to work out some simple calculations on how noise reduces with distance, understand some of the basic terms, and be able to understand what a noise consultant is telling you), then this publication is for you.

2. Some Basic Definitions

Acoustics

The science concerned with the properties of sound.

Calibration

Where an instrument is checked to determine its accuracy, in most cases this is a "field calibration" immediately before use and after a period of use on site (see section 4). A basic acoustic calibrator is used in a "field calibration" to carry out a calibration on site. A further full traceable calibration is carried out on the whole measurement system, including microphone, sound level meter and field calibrator to check the operation, usually by an external laboratory or testing service, every 1 – 2 years.

Decibel (dB)

A much misunderstood unit used for measuring the relative loudness of sound. Because the range of sound intensities and pressures is extremely wide a logarithmic scale is used (dB). Strictly speaking it is not a unit but actually a ratio. As it is a logarithmic scale decibels cannot simply be added together (such as 80 dB + 80 dB = 160 dB) instead they have to be added logarithmically (i.e. 80 dB +80 dB = 83 dB). This is covered further in section 7.

Dynamic Range

The operating range of a sound level meter or the range of sound levels that the instrument is capable of measuring. This used to a significant issue with older sound level meters which had limited ranges (often only 30 – 50 dB), leading to overloads or under-reading. Modern instruments now have much greater dynamic ranges and will often adjust the range automatically.

Frequency

In noise and acoustics the number of vibrations or pressure fluctuations per second measured in Hertz (Hz) or Kilohertz (KHz). The frequency of sound determines its pitch, i.e. low frequency sounds are low pitch, (below 1000 Hz), high frequency sounds are high pitch (above 6000 Hz). Human speech falls within the range 1000 – 6000 Hz. For the purposes of measurement and assessment, frequencies are often divided up into Octave bands and 1/3 Octave Bands.

Frequency Weighting Networks

Different frequency networks have been developed to take into account the human ears response to noise, which is not linear or equal across frequencies, but means that mid frequency sounds (1000 – 4000 Hz) are the most audible. The A weighting is the one most commonly used, though C weighting is sometimes encountered, particularly in workplace and hearing protection assessments. Other weightings do exist but are not widely used. When used in measurements the letter of the weighting network is used after the scale indicator, for example dB(A) or dBA, meaning that it is an A weighted measurement of noise in decibels. Where no weighting is applied the measurement is usually termed Linear or sometimes Z weighted (which has superseded Linear weighting).

Hearing Loss

Hearing or the sensitivity of the ear to sound reduces naturally due to ageing, but can also occur due to exposure to high levels of noise, disease or physical injury. Hearing loss due to high levels of noise exposure can be temporary (Temporary Threshold Shift) or permanent (Permanent Threshold Shift) Permanent hearing loss may occur where prolonged noise exposure has occurred, often following repeated temporary heating loss events. Hearing loss due to noise exposure always affects the high frequencies first.

Instrument Response

To iron out extremely rapid fluctuations in sound levels during measurements, different instrument response settings can be used on sound level meters; these are usually slow, fast, peak and impulse. Most environmental and occupational noise measurements are made on fast setting, but for very short term noise (e.g. gunshots) peak may be used.

LEP,d

Daily personal exposure to noise, an index defined in The Control of Noise at Work Regulations, which is calculated from the actual measured fluctuating sound pressure levels of the noise and the duration of exposure. It will have the same value as a steady or constant sound measured over the working day. It is often automatically measured by most modern sound level meters, but can be manually calculated. It is an A weighted index used in noise at work situations.

Leq or LAeq

This is the equivalent continuous sound level, an energy mean (usually A weighted) of the noise averaged over the measurement period. It can be considered as a continuous steady noise level that would have the same acoustic energy as the actual fluctuating noise measured over the period of time. Leq is widely used in environmental noise monitoring both for long term (several hours or more) and very short (less than a minute) measurements. It is usually measured directly by modern sound level meters.

The LAeq is sometimes referred to as the "average" noise but as that can be misinterpreted should always be referred to as the Leq, LAeq or Leq dBA.

Loudness

The loudness of a sound is dependant not only on the noise level (in decibels) but also the frequency of the sound. This relates to the range of human hearing which is not equal across all frequencies but is most acute in the range 1 KHz to 6 KHz. In broad terms this means a noise at a higher or lower frequency needs to be at a higher intensity (more decibels) than a sound at 1 KHz to be the same loudness to the listener. To take account of this, graphs called equal loudness curves or contours have been developed which show equal loudness across the range of human hearing for noise at the differing frequencies.

To further complicate loudness, we do not respond to noise in a linear way as sound level rises, (for example from 50 to 53 dB). A 1 dB increase in noise level is barely noticeable, a 3 db increase would be noticeable — even though it is a doubling of sound energy (see section 7), while in general terms a 10 dB increase in noise level corresponds to a doubling of loudness, i.e. noise levels need to rise by 10 dB for it to appear to be twice as loud, but is in fact a 10 fold increase in sound energy.

L10, L50, L90 – Statistical Indices

It is common for sound level measurements to be referred to or recorded as statistical indices, the most often encountered will be L10, L50 and L90, but many others may be used. L10 means the noise level which exceeded for 10% of the time over the duration of the noise measurements, L50 the noise level exceeded for 50% of the time, and L90 the level exceeded for 90% of the time. Essentially the Marker L that follows the sound or noise measurement means Level and results may be reported in the following ways: 45 dBA L90 or 45 dB LA90.

L90 is often referred to as the background noise level in the UK in environmental noise measurements.

Noise and Sound

Noise is often defined as sound which is loud, a by product or unintended consequence of the operation of plant and machinery, and or is undesired by the recipient.
Sound is an aural (hearing) sensation caused by pressure variations in the air produced by some kind of vibration. The pressure waves pass through the air (or other material) to a receiver where it is perceived. It is important to note that none of the actual particles in the air pass along from the source to the receiver; it is the energy of the disturbance that passes along as it is transmitted from one air particle to another.

Range of Human Hearing

The range of sound from low to high frequencies is extremely large, and above and below certain frequencies the human ear cannot detect sound. The exact frequency range of human hearing varies widely between people, and children can commonly hear higher frequencies inaudible to adults. Sound below the range of human hearing is called infra sound, and above the range is called ultrasound. The frequency range for humans is normally considered to be 20 Hz to 18 KHz.

Sound Level Meters

These are instruments used to measure, and sometimes record noise. They vary in design from very basic to very complex and there are British and International standards for the differing types. Instruments used in occupational and environmental noise settings should be class/type 1, which are of a higher accuracy and precision than cheaper class/type 2 meters, which are more for indicative purposes. The type and details of sound level meters used in any noise assessment must always be recorded.

3. The Effects of Noise

Noise can have a number of effects on health. These can include the more obvious ones such as hearing damage (loss) caused by exposure to loud noise, which can be temporary or permanent, and other hearing damage caused by noise such as, tinnitus ("ringing" in the ears) which can become permanent, loudness recruitment (distortion in the response to sound), and diplacusis (double hearing or sounds having different tones in each ear).

Noise exposure can be associated with annoyance, increased stress levels, cardiovascular disease and mental health implications. It can affect verbal communication at home and at the workplace, and has been associated with sleep disturbance, leading to illness. Studies have shown a range of other effects, including effects on the learning abilities of children taught in schools under busy flight paths, as well as reduced educational attainment.

While the hearing damage effects of loud noise are well understood and can be related to specific noise levels, the health impacts of the other sources may be less well correlated to noise level as other factors may be as important. These factors include, the tonal characteristics, how often and for how long it continues, the time of day and which days it occurs, whether there are any other characteristics such as impulsiveness (e.g. a dog bark) and the perceived necessity for the noise.

4. How is Noise Measured?

Noise is measured in decibels (dB) using instruments known as sound level meters There are many types of sound level meters (often referred to as SLM's). They all work in essentially the same way. Sound pressure waves or vibrations of the air are converted to an electrical signal by a microphone. Within the microphone there is a diaphragm that vibrates as a sound pressure wave impinges upon it. This is then converted into an electrical signal which is then processed by the sound level meter into an output, usually a display on the instrument, in decibels. The basic sound that is recorded by an instrument is called the Sound Pressure Level (SPL).

Most modern sound level meters cannot only display the basic Sound Pressure Level, but have the ability to carry out a range of processing of the measured signal such as the application of frequency weighting networks, altering the averaging or response time (Fast or Slow response) carrying out statistical analysis, L10, L50 L90, calculating Equivalent Continuous Noise Level (LAeq), and commonly the ability to record the noise onto internal memory or memory cards. Some instruments can also carry out frequency analysis, such as Octave Band or 1/3 Octave Band analysis.

There are different classes of sound level meters; the main ones that will be found are Type/Class 1 and Type/Class 2 instruments. Type/Class 1 instruments are the most accurate and are usually used in environmental investigations and research applications. Type/Class 2 are mainly used in industrial settings commonly for occupational noise (Noise at Work) and more indicative monitoring.

For measuring noise in workplaces, particularly for mobile workforces or where the noise level may vary widely, small noise dosimeters are available which can be worn by a worker as they carry out their duties and these can measure the total noise exposure of the wearer over the period worn.

Sometimes you will see the term Sound Power Level (SWL) used, commonly on machinery where it might be on a label fixed onto a piece of potentially noisy plant or equipment such as a chainsaw or shredder. Sound Power Level can be most easily defined as the absolute sound level (or sound energy) generated by the source at the source, with no correction for any other factors. Sound Pressure Levels (SPL) on the other hand are measurements of sound, and as measurements are dependent on the distance from the source, absorption by surfaces, reflections or reverberation etc, it would otherwise be necessary to specify these factors on the labels.

5. Making Sound Level Measurements

Making Sound level measurements is not as simple as it might first seem. There are many different parameters and permutations to noise measurements depending on what you are trying to measure and why. In some cases Legislation may define how you make your noise measurements, such as the type of instruments to use, how they are to be set up, measurement location, the conditions under which you make the measurements etc. In other cases British or International standards may exist, which although may not be obligatory are often considered good practice to follow, or even essential in some cases.

The most important point to remember if making noise level measurements, or if reviewing others work, is that there must be a clear and easy to follow record of exactly how the measurements were made, a clear rational on why the approach chosen was used, that particular instrument was chosen, that that particular location monitored, why the dates and times were chosen, and any assumptions made. This means that measurements are repeatable by someone else, and even if the actual results are subject to dispute, at least both parties can agree on methodology.

In any report that is produced, it is important that the experience and qualifications of the author and the person or people carrying out the assessment are included. There are many variables to consider and it may be essential to be able to indicate to a court or in a planning application that the people carrying out any noise assessment are technically competent and have the necessary experience of making noise level measurements "in the field".

So how do you actually carry out a noise measurement? Well, as mentioned above this depends on why and what you are measuring but there are 5 basic steps (See sections 21, 22 and 23 for more details on how to carry out noise assessments):

1. **The first step in any noise monitoring exercise is to find out exactly what you are measuring and why.**

2. **Then find out background information to give you an understanding of the issues or problems you might encounter when making any measurements, and where measurements are best made.**

3. **Then plan your noise measurement exercise, this is a stage which is worth spending time on to be able to make the most effective and appropriate measurements.**

4. **Make your measurements in line with your plan and keep records of what you do and observe, remembering that although your results can and may be challenged or subject to dispute, detailed records that you make at the time are a true reflection of what you observed and therefore cannot easily be challenged.**

5. **Finally review and process your data, and write up your results. Include in your report details from the notes you took, maps and plans, any assumptions made etc.**

6. What are Frequencies, Octave Bands and 1/3 Octaves?

Noise is made up of a wide variety of sounds or tones, some of higher pitch some of lower. Higher pitch being higher frequencies, lower pitch lower frequencies. The frequency of sound is measured in Hertz (Hz) and Kilohertz (KHz) (1000 Hz = 1 KHz) and a Hertz is the number of oscillations (or sound waves) per second.

The range of human hearing across the frequencies is very large form 20 Hz to around 20 KHz. To make measurements and assessments of noise more manageable, especially where examining frequency, it is common to group or break the noise up into bands, usually Octave Bands and 1/3 Octave Bands. It is possible to monitor very narrow frequency bands (often called narrow band frequency analysis), but this is used less often. Narrow band frequency analysis is useful when looking for a particular tone, such as when a specific noise is being investigated (for example, an annoying hum).

Octave Bands are an internationally agreed set of bands of frequencies that include all the noise from the individual frequencies within that range. They are referred to as the midpoint of the range after rounding, for example the 250 Hz Octave Band covers the range 176 Hz to 353 Hz.

The purpose of both Octave Bands and 1/3 Octave Bands is to allow some assessment of the frequency of the noise under investigation so that particular characteristics can be identified in environmental noise investigations, or particular problems anticipated in noise level predictions, for example in planning applications. They can be further used to assess the effectiveness of sound insulation measures and materials and in devising appropriate hearing protection in workplaces.

TABLE 1 THE OCTAVE BANDS

Octave Band (Hz)	Frequency range (Hz)	Pitch
31.5	22	Low Pitch
31.5	44	Low Pitch
63	44	Low Pitch
63	88	Low Pitch
125	88	Low Pitch
125	176	Low Pitch
250	176	Low Pitch
250	353	Low Pitch
500	353	Mid Range
500	707	Mid Range
1000	707	Mid Range
1000	1414	Mid Range
2000	1414	Mid Range
2000	2825	Mid Range
4000	2825	Mid Range
4000	5650	Mid Range
8000	5650	High Pitch
8000	11300	High Pitch
16000	11300	High Pitch
16000	22500	High Pitch

TABLE 2 THE 1/3 OCTAVE BANDS ARE A FURTHER SUBDIVISION OF THE OCTAVE BANDS

Octave Band (Hz)	1/3 Octave Band (Hz)
31.5	25
	31.5
	44
63	50
	63
	80
125	100
	125
	160
250	200
	250
	315
500	400
	500
	630
1000	800
	1000
	1250
2000	1600
	2000
	2500
4000	3150
	4000
	5000
8000	6300
	8000
	10000
16000	12500
	16000
	20000

7. How Do I Add Noise Levels Together?

Noise levels in decibels are logarithmic scales of sound energy and so cannot be added together arithmetically i.e. 80 dB + 80 dB **does not** equal 160 dB. Instead it is necessary to add them together logarithmically, effectively adding the energy represented by the levels together, not the value of the levels themselves. The following formulas and examples show how noise levels are added or subtracted. There are also tables or simple charts that can be used to provide an approximation that is good enough for most basic purposes.

7.1 To Add Two or More Noise Levels Together Using a Formula

Formula SPL = 10 log($10^{(L1/10)}$ + $10^{(L2/10)}$)

E.g. Two noise levels, one of 50 dB and one of 47 dB

$$\text{SPL} = 10 \log(10^{(50/10)} + 10^{(47/10)})$$
$$= 10 \log(10^5 + 10^{4.7})$$
$$= 10 \log(100000 + 50118)$$
$$= 10 \log(150118)$$
$$= 10 \times 5.1764$$
$$= 51.8 \text{ dB}$$

The same formula can be used for adding more than two sources of noise

7.2 To Add Two Noise Levels Using the Table or Chart Method

To use the chart or table method, work out the difference between noise levels, and use Figure 1 or Table 3 to add the corresponding figure from the table or chart to the **higher** of the noise levels.

For example adding 50 dB and 47 dB.

The difference between them is 3 dB. From Table 3 the corresponding number is 2 dB which is added to 50 dB to give us 52 dB.

TABLE 3 TABLE FOR ADDING NOISE LEVELS TOGETHER

Difference between 2 noise levels in dB	Add to **Higher** Level dB
0	3
1	2.5
2	2
3	2
4	1.5
5	1
6	1
7	1
8	0.5
9	0.5
10 or more	0

FIGURE 1 CHART TO ADD NOISE LEVELS TOGETHER

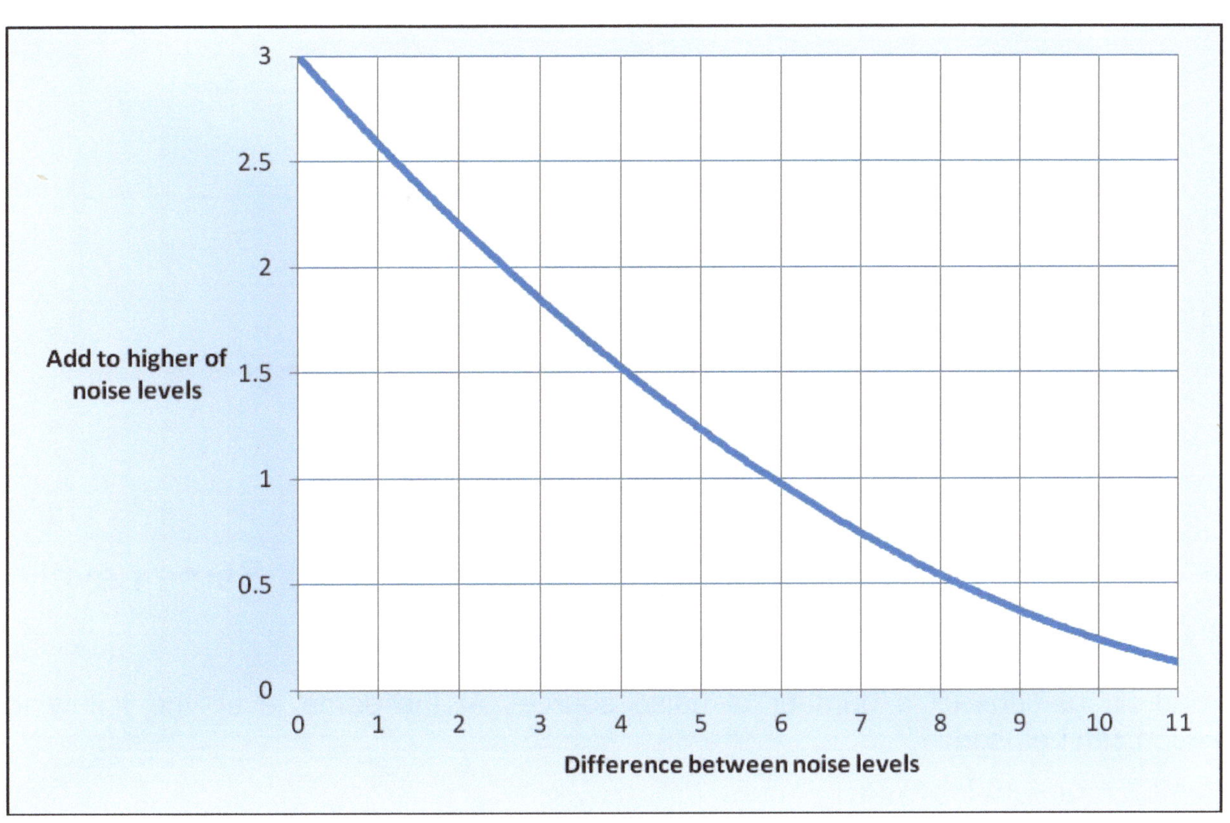

7.3   To Add Several Noise Levels Using the Table or Chart Method

To quickly add several noise levels together avoiding calculations, you can do the following:

For example: To add the following noise levels, perhaps measured from a number of machines operated individually, to give an overall noise level,

52 dB, 69 dB, 52 dB, 60 dB, 64 dB.

First put them in ascending order, then pair them up and using Table 3 add to each other, don't worry about any without a pair. Then add the totals from the pairs using Table 3 or Figure 1 and bring in any unpaired numbers, continue until there is only one number left and that will be your overall noise level.

FIGURE 2 ADDING UP NOISE LEVELS USING THE CHART OR TABLE METHOD

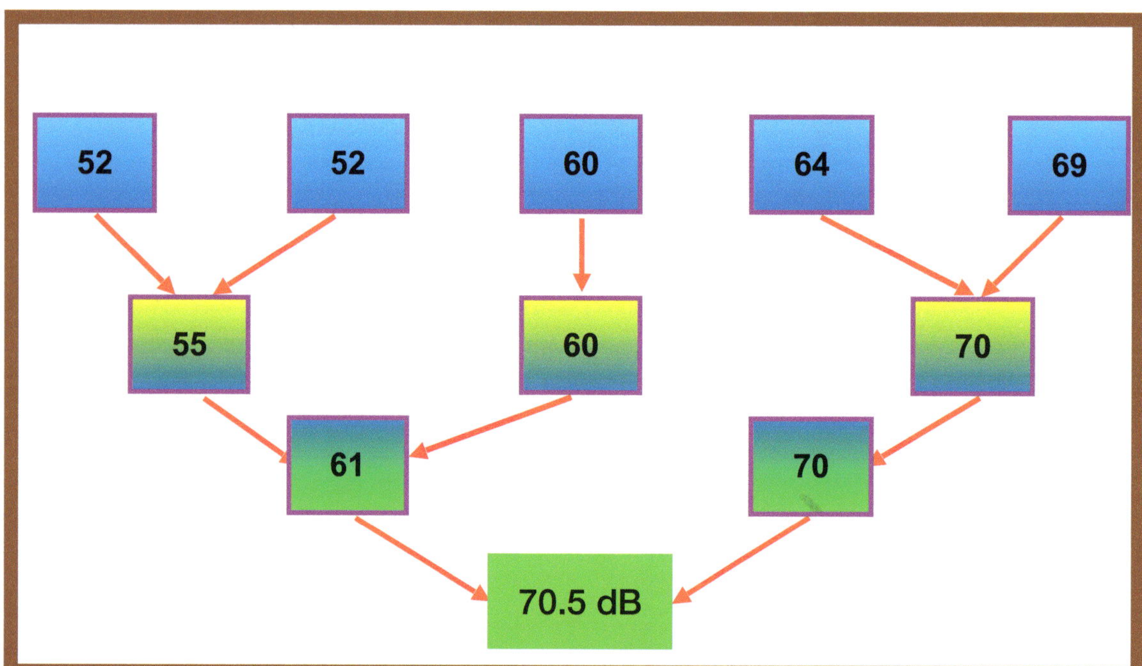

7.4 To Add Several Noise Sources Which are at the Same Level, Formula Method

To add up or subtract a number of noise sources at the same level, the following equation can be used:

SPL = L1 + or − 10 log(n_1/n_2)

Where L1 is noise level

For example what will be the noise levels from five machines all at 60 dB?

SPL = 60 + 10 log(5/1)

SPL = 60 + 10 log(5)

SPL = 60 + 10 x 0.698

SPL = 60 + 6.9 = 67 dB

If two machines out of the five are switched off what will be the level?

SPL = 67 + 10 log(3/5) (i.e. 3 of the 5 machines are still switched on)

SPL = 67 + 10 log(0.6)

SPL = 67 + 10 x - 0.221

SPL = 67 + (- 2.2)

SPL = 67 – 2 = 65 dB

7.5   Rounding of Noise Levels from Calculations

In carrying out noise calculations, for the vast majority of purposes calculations should be rounded to the nearest whole dB. Sound level meters are rarely more than 0.5 dB accurate and as the human ear cannot distinguish below a 1 dB difference in level, there is little point in being more precise than 1 dB.

8. How Does Noise Reduce Over Distance?

As sound waves pass through the air from the source to a receiver, the noise level reduces. There are, however different reductions due to distance depending upon the type of source, the type of ground over which the noise passes, weather conditions and the effects of any barriers, obstacles, or reflections. Different frequencies will also attenuate at different rates due to atmospheric absorption, though in most cases the effect is minor compared to other reduction factors and can be safely discounted, unless distances from the sources are greater than 500 metres. While in practice every situation will be different, there are some basic rules that apply.

Noise sources are generally considered a point source or a line source. It is important to be clear how the noise is being considered in any calculation or prediction.

> ➢ A line source is a source that no matter how far away you are, still appears large horizontally, such as a road where the noise comes from traffic along the road length.

➢ A point source is an individual noise source, such as an individual machine or group of machines. In most cases it is clear how the noise should be classified, but sometimes it is not so obvious, and becomes a matter of judgement.

Occasionally very large noise sources will be found, that are large both vertically and horizontally; this might be a very large factory building where the noise emanates equally through the building walls. This would be termed a plane source, and such a source may behave partly as a line source and partly as a point source, depending on distance from it. This situation is relatively uncommon and will not be considered further here.

8.1   Reduction from a Point Source

Sound from a point source radiates equally in all directions, with the source forming the centre of a ball or sphere, which grows in size as the sound wave travels. As the sphere becomes larger as it grows in size, this means the sound energy is spread out over a wider area. As we hear and measure the noise energy at a receiver point, as the distance increases from the source there is less sound energy to measure, thus the sound pressure level decreases. From a point source the reduction in noise level is a 6 dB reduction per doubling of distance, for example 10 metres to 20 metres (known as the inverse square law).

There is a relatively simple equation that can be used to work out the reduction in noise as distance increases. It depends on:

 a) Knowing the noise level at a precise distance from the source,

 And

b) Knowing the distance from the source at the location you are interested in

Formula = **SPL = L1 + 20 log(d1/d2)**

Where L1 is noise level

d1 is original distance

d2 is new distance

For example

We measure a noise level of 63 dB at 25 metres from the source. We then need to know what it will be at 50 metres where we want to build a new house.

> **SPL = 63 + 20 log(25/50)**
>
> **= 63 + 20 log(0.5)**
>
> **= 63 + 20 X - 0.301**
>
> **= 63 - 6**
>
> **= 57 dB at the new house**

This equation can also be used to work out the effect of reducing distance from a known measurement point to a noise source, the d1 and d2 just need to be reversed (i.e. d2 over d1).

> **Note**
>
> While this calculation is correct for noise levels from a point source and distance, the noise at the receiver location or new distance can be influenced by other factors, such as the nature of the ground over which the noise travels and it may be necessary to take this into account (see section 8.3)

8.2   Reduction from a Line Source

Sound from a line source radiates along a line, and thus it forms a cylinder with the source at the centre and the cylinder becoming larger as the sound waves travels. As the sound energy is spread over a wider area, as the cylinder become larger as distance from the source increases, the noise level we hear and measure at the receiver point reduces with increasing distance.   From a line source the reduction in sound energy is a 3 dB reduction as distance doubles, for example from 100 metres to 200 metres.

There is a relatively simple equation that can be used to work out the reduction in noise as distance increases. It depends on:

 a) Knowing the noise level at a precise distance from the source,

 And

b) Knowing the distance from the source at the location you are interested in.

Formula = **SPL = L1 + 10 log(d1/d2)**

Where L1 is noise level

d1 is original distance

d2 is new distance

For example

We measure a noise level of 63 dB at 25 metres from a busy road. We then need to know what it will be at 50 metres where we want to build a new house.

> **SPL = 63 + 10 log(25/50)**
>
> **= 63 + 10 log(0.5)**
>
> **= 63 + 10 X - 0.301**
>
> **=63 - 3**
>
> **= 60 dB at the new house**

This equation can also be used to work out the effect of reducing distance from a known measurement point to a noise source, the d1 and d2 just need to be reversed (i.e. d2 over d1).

Note

While this calculation is correct for noise levels from a line source and distance, the noise at the receiver location or new distance can be influenced by other factors, such as the nature of the ground over which the noise travels and it may be necessary to take this into account (see section 8.3).

8.3   Effects of Different Types of Ground

As noise passes over the ground there are a range of effects that may occur, (reflections and absorptions), and these may affect the measured noise level at the receiver point, leading to differing results from those that can be calculated in section 8.1 and 8.2.

Ground reflection occurs in all measurements made in the field from both line and point sources, and this can increase noise levels at the measurement position. The effect may be particularly noticed from a point source where the 6 dB reduction due to doubling of distance may not be observed in practice, especially where the sound passes over hard reflective surfaces, such a wide tarmac road or concrete yard. However if the calculations are based on measurements made at known distances over the same type of surface, the measurements already include the effect of ground reflection and thus this effect can in most cases simply be ignored (the effect of the ground reflection would be a 3 dB increase as half the energy is reflected upwards).

Ground absorption can provide some reduction in noise level. Soft or rough ground, such as rough grassland, can have a measurable effect particularly over larger distances. It may be appropriate in some circumstances to take account of this in calculations by adding an additional factor, or possibly by making measurements over a range of distances over the ground in question. There are various formula that can be used from the literature, but the following rule of thumb formula could be used if the noise is broadband in nature (i.e. not particularly high or low frequency and includes a wide spectrum of frequencies). This rule of thumb can also be used to account for atmospheric absorption in some instances, such as where the noise is broadband in nature and does not contain any particular tones or noticeable frequencies.

Formula = **SPL = L1 + 26 log(d1/d2)**

Where L1 is noise level

26 is used instead of 20 log to make an allowance for significant ground absorption

d1 is original distance

d2 is new distance

For example

We measure a noise level of 63 dB at 25 metres from a point source. We then need to know what it will be at 50 metres where we want to build a new house, where the ground in-between is soft rough grassland.

> **SPL = 63 + 26 log(25/50)**
>
> **= 63 + 26 log(0.5)**
>
> **= 63 + 26 X - 0.301**
>
> **= 63 – 7.8**
>
> **= 55 dB at the new house**

This equation can also be used to work out the effect of reducing distance from a known measurement point to a noise source, the d1 and d2 just need to be reversed (i.e. d2 over d1).

> **Note**
>
> If any noise barrier or fence is likely to be in place or used, any ground absorption effects, calculations or assumptions should be disregarded.

9. How Do Noise Barriers Work?

Noise barriers, at their most acoustically simple, are a physical barrier between the noise and the receiver. The term is usually used in relation to outside barriers, such as those that might be seen alongside a busy road. Assessing the effectiveness of noise barriers can be complex depending on the noise source and frequency. However there are some basic principles that apply.

Noise barriers essentially work by increasing the path length that the noise has to travel to reach the receiver.

FIGURE 3 HOW A NOISE BARRIER WORKS

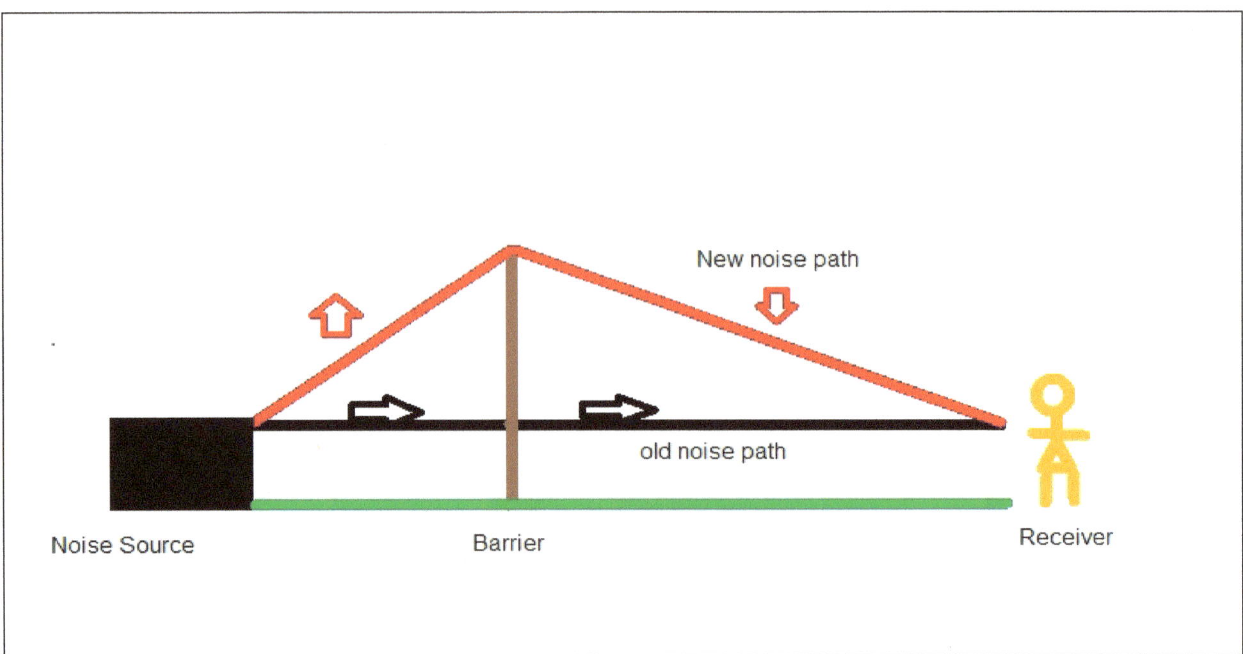

To be effective a barrier has to meet the following principles:

- It must break the line of sight between the receiver and the source.

- It is most effective when close to the source or the receiver, as this increases effective path length the most, and is least effective midway between the two.

- A barrier must be of sufficient length to prevent or significantly reduce noise passing around the ends of the barrier reaching the receiver.

- A barrier must be of a material that will prevent noise passing through it. In most cases the denser the material the better it will perform, where a lightweight material is used it should be capable of reducing sound passing through it by at least 10 dB.

- There must be no holes or gaps in a barrier, or between the barrier and the ground.

Where a barrier just breaks the line of sight to the source in most cases a 5 dB reduction will be achieved, but in terms or human response to noise, this will not appear significant to a receiver. Where a noise barrier totally blocks the line of sight, as a rule of thumb a 10 dB reduction will be achieved.

10. The Myth about Trees and Hedges

There is a belief amongst much of the public that trees and hedges are effective barriers against noise. Whilst it is true they may have minor effects, with the exception of specially designed living or green acoustic barriers or hedges, their effect is negligible acoustically. This is because they do not normally have the required density to absorb noise to any great effect. There may be some benefit in higher frequency or low frequency noise reduction from thick belts of trees (in excess of 50 metres thick), but in the mid range frequencies they may be of little effect over and above normal attenuation over soft rough ground (see section 8). If it is thought appropriate to make any allowance for trees and hedges in any calculation or prediction, then a reduction of no more 1-2 dB may be appropriate.

The main effect of trees and hedges may be psychological, in removing a noise source from view, it may be perceived as less intrusive in a community, and thus be less subject to complaint. In addition the noise that is caused by wind passing through a tree or hedge screen may provide a masking noise that may make a particular noise source less apparent.

11. Weather and its Effects

The weather can have effects (sometimes very significant effects) on noise levels and the propagation of sound. However the possibility of other effects, not just to do with the sound energy from the source in question should also be considered. For example high winds can raise noise levels by causing rustling of leaves on trees and bushes, rain may increase noise from roads by making surfaces wet and increasing tyre noise leading to the masking of a noise under investigation, whilst fog or snow may reduce background or road noise, not due to any acoustic effects, but by reducing the number of cars travelling as people avoid travelling or travel at slower speeds.

Wind will have an effect on noise in the following ways. Upwind from a noise source the effect of the wind can be to refract (bend) the sound upwards, leading to a reduction in sound level at this location. Downwind the wind refracts the sound downwards leading to an increase in sound level. This effect occurs because the wind speed will vary according to height, with the slowest speeds near the ground with greater speeds higher up.(See figure 4)

Air temperature and temperature inversions can have effects on noise propagation. The speed of sound through the air depends upon temperature and pressure. Whilst atmospheric pressure change is not significant in most cases, temperature does affect the speed of sound at ground level and as temperature rises the speed of sound also rises.

FIGURE 4 REFRACTION OF SOUND WAVES BY WIND

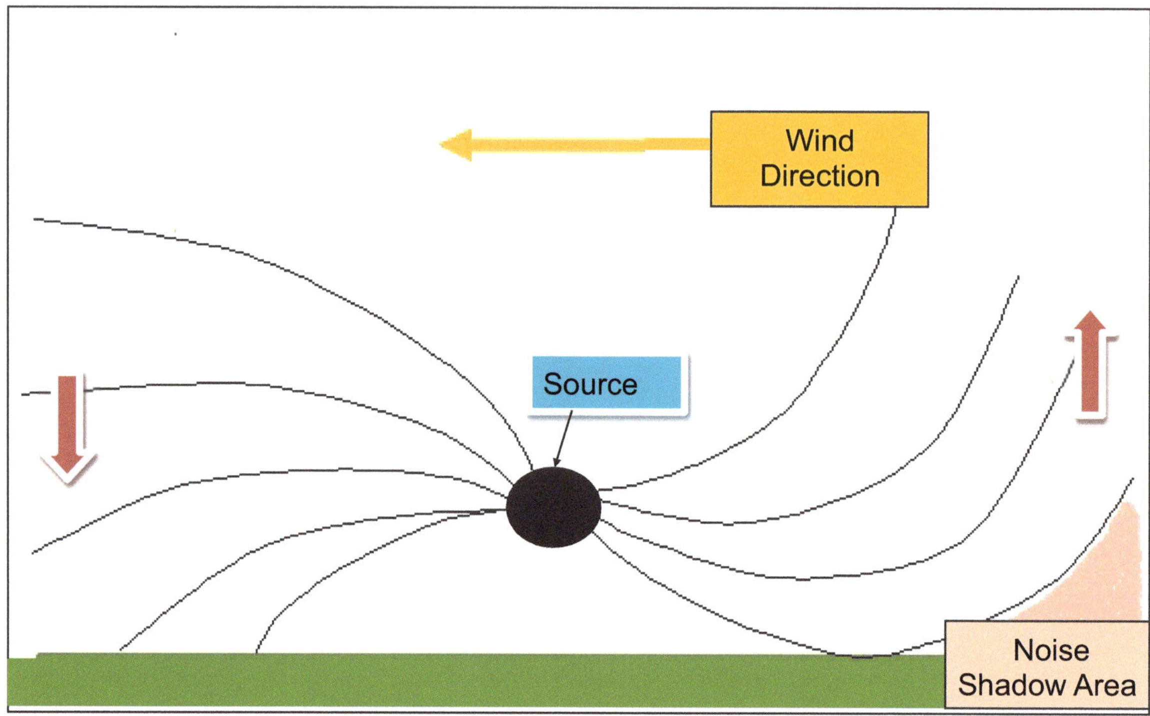

Normally, in what are called lapse conditions, temperature falls as height increases, and this has the effect of refracting (bending) sound upwards away from the ground. The effects of temperature inversions, where the air at higher levels is warmer than at ground level, leads to differing sound speeds and can lead to the sound being refracted towards the ground giving rise to the effect of the sound appearing to travel further (see figure 5). This is the effect that can sometimes be noted on during calm conditions on cool summer evenings around sunset or at sunrise on winter mornings.

In practice it can be difficult to judge these effects when making noise level measurements and where possible windy days or periods with temperature inversions should be avoided. This may not always be possible and reinforces the need to make careful records of conditions during any measurement exercise so that there is potential to take account of these effects in any subsequent assessment.

FIGURE 5 REFRACTION OF SOUND WAVES DUE TO TEMPERATURE INVERSION

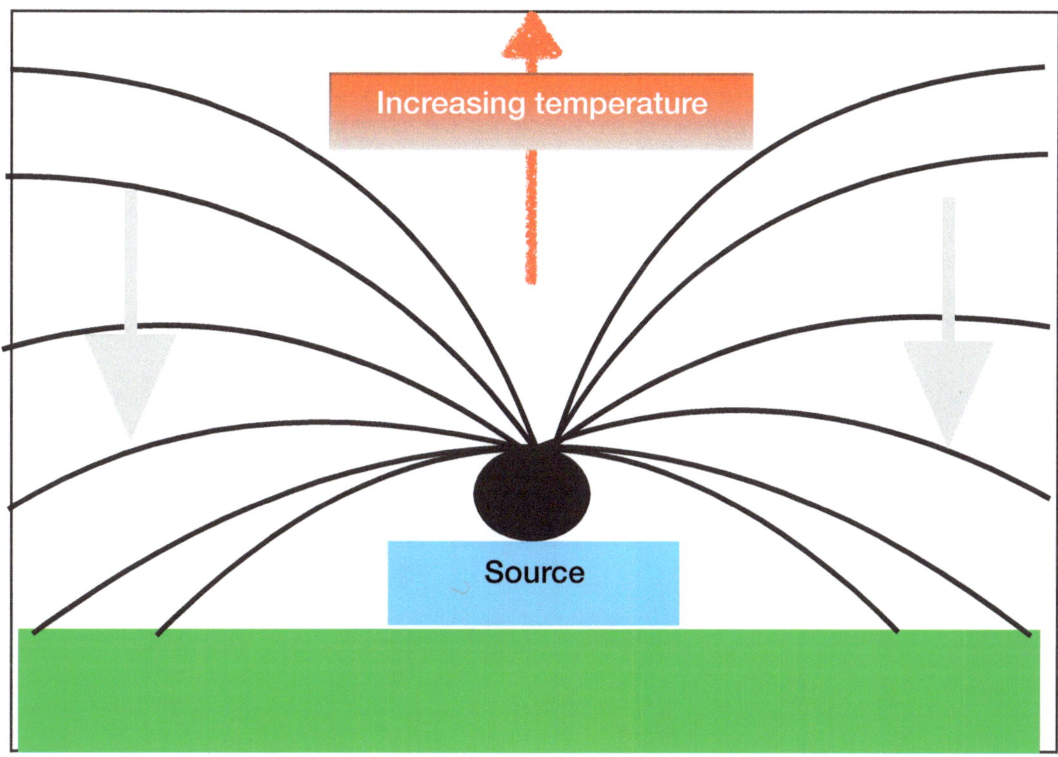

12. Sound Insulation

The term sound insulation normally means either preventing noise from escaping from the source, such as by an enclosure around a machine, or preventing sound entering an area where we wish to reduce or control noise levels, for example in a bedroom of a house. Essentially both techniques involve placing a barrier between the noise and the receiver.

When sound waves in the air meet a wall or partition, some of the sound energy is reflected from the wall; some is absorbed by the wall, some passes into the wall and travels along it, and some passes through it and is retransmitted on the other side.(See figure 6)

FIGURE 6 SOUND WAVES MEETING A WALL OR BARRIER

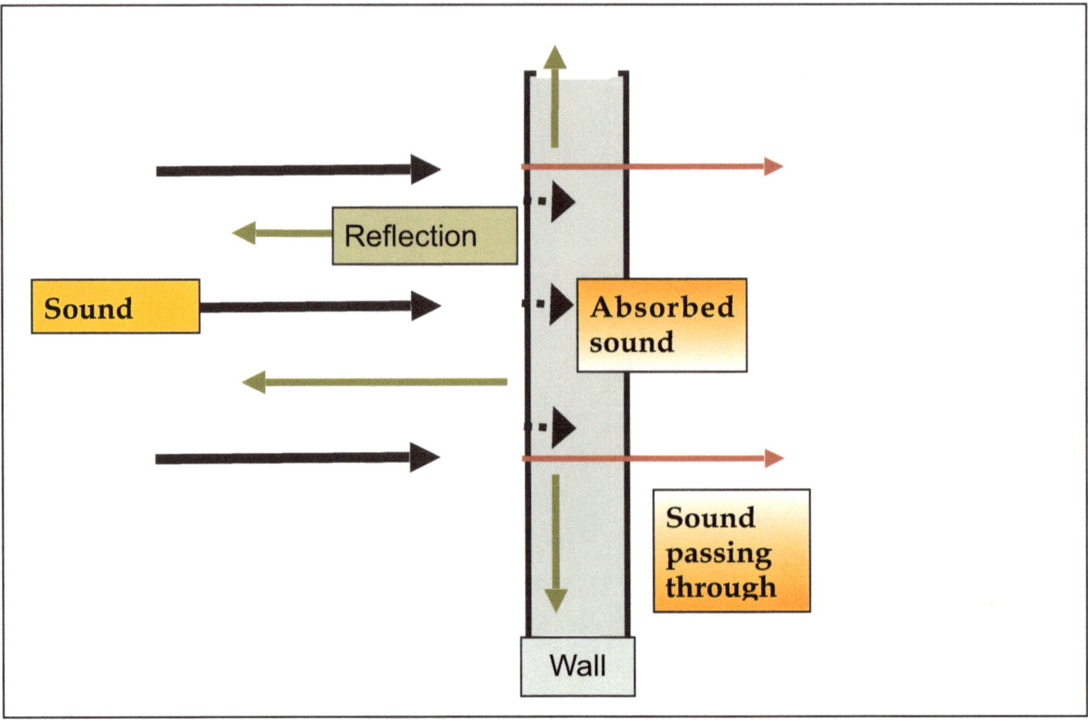

In terms of effectiveness of sound insulation, one of the most important factors is the mass of the wall or partition, the greater the mass the greater the insulating properties. The frequency of the sound is also important, high frequency sounds are less easily transmitted by the wall or partition, while low frequency sounds are more easily transmitted. There is a basic calculation (the mass law of sound insulation) that can be used to assess the effectiveness of a partition or wall of known mass against differing frequencies of sound.

TABLE 4 THE MASS LAW OF SOUND INSULATION

Sound Reduction = 20 x log(M x f) - 45 dB

Where:

M is the weight of the partition/wall in Kg/m^3

f is the frequency in Hz

Overall, the doubling of the mass of the partition gives a 6 dB increase in sound insulation, and the partition becomes 6 dB more effective per octave increase in frequency.

The stiffness of the partition or wall is also important. Where the wall is of high stiffness (think of a biscuit tin with a stiff metal base), it may have the effect of resonating at certain frequencies and this may have the effect of reducing the sound reduction properties significantly. The application of a damping material can reduce this resonance and this increases the effectiveness of the barrier.

While we can increase the density and thickness of a wall, or reduce stiffness by adding a damping material, to increase insulation, another way is to construct a second wall or partition alongside the existing structure. To gain greatest effect the second wall should not be in contact with the first wall, if possible, as any joins will provide a path for the sound energy to travel through. In addition the air in the cavity between the walls may resonate, though this can be controlled by use of an absorbent material such as rockwool. The effect of the second wall will improve the insulation, but will **not** double the effectiveness of the single wall.

The Sound Reduction Index of sound insulating materials (a laboratory test of sound reduction properties at 1/3 Octave or Octave bands) may be provided by the manufacturers in many cases and these can be used to provide an indication of effectiveness. This can be particularly useful where a particular frequency is shown to be an issue, for example by measurements, allowing the material likely to be of greatest effectiveness to be chosen for that particular frequency. In other cases a single figure may be given of the sound insulation properties (often an Rw value) which provides a good indicator of general effectiveness, with the greater the Rw the greater the insulation.

TABLE 5 SOME TYPICAL SOUND REDUCTION INDEX VALUES FOR MATERIALS

Material	Octave Band Hz						
	63	125	250	500	1000	2000	4000
Brick wall	29	34	36	41	51	58	60
Window with 4mm glass	20	20	22	27	30	28	26
Double glazed window 6mm glass/ 12mm air gap/ 6mm glass	19	23	25	27	31	34	37
3mm sheet steel	16	21	27	33	38	39	33
6mm aluminium sheet	13	19	25	30	36	30	32

Note

In any sound insulation, joints and openings in the barrier will be weak points allowing transmission of sound, and sound insulation is only as good as its weakest point. Therefore, where possible joints and openings should be avoided. Failure of sound insulation in practice to achieve its predicted sound reduction is often caused by such weak points.

12.1 Sound Absorbency

In addition to insulation properties of any wall or barrier, another approach to reduce noise within a room or enclosure is to improve the absorbency of the sound energy. Sound energy is reflected back off surfaces, as well as passing through and being absorbed by them. If we can reduce the reflections back into the space by increasing the absorbency of the surfaces this can reduce noise levels within the room or area. Absorbent materials are usually soft heavy materials like carpet underlay or cork tiles, while smooth concrete, glass and ceramic tiles have very low absorbent properties. The Noise Reduction Coefficient (NRC) measures how well materials absorb noise in a scale of 0 to 1 where 1 is 100% absorbency and 0 is none.

13. How do Silencers Work?

Silencers are used where there is a flow of air or exhaust gas through a duct/tube either into or from a machine or process. The machine or process may be inherently noisy, such as with combustion plant (e.g. a car engine), or it may be that there is a fan or other plant used to provide or increase airflow and this produces noise. Noise emitted from fans and duct/pipework is a common cause of complaint and thus it is common for silencers to be fitted to reduce noise levels.

Silencers consist of a device fitted to inlets and outlets to reduce the noise emitted from the outlet while allowing the air or gas to pass through with as little hindrance as possible. There are essentially 2 types: Reactive and Dissipative or Absorptive.

Note

Fan noise is often the result of air turbulence caused by the fan, which is influenced by the speed of the fan blade tips and the number of blades. Before embarking on the installation of silencers on a problem fan it is worth seeing if reducing the fan speed (if technically possible) may alter or reduce particular tones. In addition checking that the fan is properly maintained (for example squeaking bearings), is not clogged up or otherwise damaged, should be carried out as this may address many fan noise issues.

13.1 Dissipative or Absorptive

These are the simplest type of silencers and consist of sound absorbing material placed into the duct. In their simplest form they just consist of a lining on the inside of the duct, but to increase sound absorbency, splitter silencers are frequently used. These are where the flow is split into channels lined with absorbent material, increasing the surface area available for absorbency. Generally, the narrower the channels and the thicker the absorbency the better the noise reduction. However, by narrowing the gas flow too much, increased noise can be created as the gas has to increase in velocity to pass through the silencer.

13.2 Reactive Silencers

These use acoustic principles to reflect the sound back towards the source or otherwise interfere with the sound wave, which has the effect of reducing noise levels. In their simplest form they may be just an expanded section of ductwork, but more complex forms can include several expansion chambers in series and other techniques. Reactive silencers can be "tuned" to address specific frequencies or tones, particularly useful where measurement or manufacturers data shows that a particular tone may give rise to disturbance and complaints.

13.3 Correct Locations of Silencers

To be most effective a silencer has to be correctly positioned and installed. A silencer should be located at least 3 – 4 duct diameters away from a bend or junction. The closer the silencer is to the source the more effective it will be; however if it too close to the fan or plant giving rise to the noise, increased back pressure may result in increased noise levels. The silencer will need to be close enough to the source to ensure that the noise is controlled before travelling along the length of the duct, as otherwise it may break out from the ductwork walls.

13.4 Other Considerations When Using Silencers

Silencers may need to be cleaned and inspected, so should be located in accessible areas.

Any dust, grease or particulate in the airflow may be abrasive to the silencer, or clog up porous absorbent material, whilst moisture may cause corrosion.

The temperature of the gas flow should be considered, high temperatures may prevent the use of certain absorbent materials.

Noise may still be emitted from the ductwork itself before the silencer. The use of damping and stiffening materials on the ductwork may be needed, as may anti-vibration mountings on ductwork fixings to prevent sound transmission to other surfaces.

14. Noise Legislation

There is a large volume of legislation around noise, covering everything from the noise from vehicles and machinery standards, sound insulation, to planning, nuisance, antisocial behaviours and health and safety. It would be a large publication indeed that covered all of his legislation, but here are listed some of the most important Acts of Parliament and Regulations that are most commonly encountered when dealing with noise.

- Environmental Protection Act 1990
- Control of Pollution Act 1974
- Noise Act 1996
- Pollution Prevention and Control Act 1999 and the Environmental Permitting Regulations 2016
- Clean Neighbourhoods and Environment Act 2005
- Anti-social Behaviour, Crime and Policing Act 2014
- Noise Insulation Regulations 1975
- Health & Safety at Work Regulations 1974
- Control of Noise at Work Regulations 2005

It is important when referring to or using any legislation that the most up to date version is used which incorporates any amendments that have been made. Legislation is constantly being updated and is subject to change. All of the legislation is available online at Legislation.gov.uk (https://www.legislation.gov.uk) and legislation on this site is usually kept up to date with any amendments.

There are in addition to the legislation, some Statutory Codes of Practice concerning certain noise sources. These are specified in law and include model aircraft noise , ice cream vans and construction sites. It was originally intended that there would be a range of these Statutory Codes of Practice, but in the event very few were ever issued, and of those that were produced, some are out of date.

15. Noise Nuisance, Complaints and Annoyance

Noise can cause considerable disturbance and can result in complaints to the authorities. However it is important not to confuse noise nuisance, noise complaints and noise annoyance.

15.1 Noise Complaint

A person may complain of noise for a number of reasons, sometimes very little to do with the sound they are experiencing. On occasion, the complaint about noise will actually be the result of a dispute between people, or dislike of a nearby factory or activity. In this case any local noise that is deemed loud or unnecessary will result in complaint, whether in fact it originates from the alleged source or not, and whether it is loud or not. In some cases a noise may be complained about that either may not actually exist, being the result of some audiological disease or mental health issue; whilst in other cases the person may have particularly sensitive hearing and be noticing frequencies not audible to most people.

15.2 Noise Annoyance

The response to a noise can be very subjective, and what will cause annoyance to one person will not be noticed by another. The necessity for a noise may also result in differing annoyance criteria, noise that is perceived as being in the public good, such as train noise, may provoke less annoyance and disturbance than noise from a factory at the same level. Noise annoyance also depends on factors such as the time of day, frequency or tone, type of noise, duration, impulsiveness, unpredictability etc. A dog barking is a noise that attracts attention and can cause considerable distress, even though measurements may demonstrate it is not especially loud. It is the unpredictability, tone, and short term nature of the barking that causes complaint and persons being affected by it can find themselves waiting for the next bark to occur.

15.3 Noise Nuisance

Noise nuisance is a term that is largely misunderstood by the public. To a member of the public any noise that is annoying is likely to be a "nuisance" and therefore a noise nuisance. To noise professionals and Environmental Health staff a noise nuisance is likely to be looked at in terms of Statutory Noise Nuisance, and this is different.

A Statutory Noise Nuisance is a nuisance that is defined in law, currently by the Environmental Protection Act 1990 Section 79. It is a noise that is emitted from premises or vehicles machinery or equipment in the street that unreasonably interferes with another person's enjoyment of their land and property.

See http://www.legislation.gov.uk/ukpga/1990/43/contents

A Statutory Nuisance is quite a high test in that case law has established it does not cover minor annoyances, but instead the level of disturbance has to be significant to a persons or group of people who are normal and reasonable (the man on the Clapham omnibus). Case law has also established that it relates to the nature and character of the area, and this can seem unfair, for example, in high noise areas a noise causing complaint may not be out of character for the area and therefore may not be a nuisance, whilst in a quiet area it may be more apparent and thus might be a Statutory Nuisance.

In more recent years legislation has offered a potential alternative approach where noise is not at the threshold necessary to be a Statutory Nuisance but still causes distress to a neighbourhood by being antisocial. This is discussed further in Section 15.4.

In England and Wales there is no specific noise level to establish a noise nuisance, a Local Authority will look at a range of factors including subjectively how loud, time of day, tonal characteristics, and impact on a recipient of the noise , etc. There is no need in law for sound level measurements to be made by an investigating authority, as it is the opinion of the authorised investigating officer based on experience and local knowledge that is most important. However noise level measurement may be made to confirm the officer's opinion, help identify the source and to identify tones and patterns of time and duration. Where noise levels measurements are made by Local Authority officers to assist in determining nuisance, it is important that the officers are competent to use the equipment and familiar with the assessment of measured levels.

Noise level measurements may be particularly helpful in nuisance investigations when dealing with commercial or industrial premises. They can:

a) confirm trends in noise levels;

b) be used in comparison with background noise levels;

c) be used to assess the effect of any technical measures taken to reduce levels;

d) potentially identify the particular source of a problem noise on a large site with many potential sources, by frequency analysis or switching plant on and off and seeing effect on levels;

e) allow the comparison of levels against objective annoyance or sleep disturbance criteria;

f) be compared against manufacturers data for plant and machinery noise levels or similar sites, to assess whether noise is normal for that type of operation or plant/ equipment.

It is not a criminal offence to cause a Statutory Noise Nuisance and there is no automatic fine or penalty. However, under the Noise Act 1996 there is a procedure not greatly different to an automatic fine relating to night time noise from domestic and licensed premises (pubs, bars and clubs), see below.

If a Statutory Noise Nuisance is established, a Local Authority is under a statutory duty to serve a Notice (an Abatement Notice) on the person responsible or owner or occupier of the premises requiring them to abate the nuisance. An offence is only committed if the person or business fails to comply with the Notice.

The Noise Act 1996, as amended, has introduced a different test and procedure for noise from domestic property and licensed premises. If noise from an adjoining property is emitted at a level that exceeds a "permitted level" of 10 dBA above the background inside the complainants property (measured over a period of not more than 5 minutes) then the Local Authority can serve a warning notice or the persons or premises responsible, which if not complied with can result in a fixed penalty notice served at the time and in a prosecution later.

Note

There is considerable case law on Statutory Nuisance and the reader who wishes to investigate Statutory Noise Nuisance Law in more detail should refer to the large amount of available literature.

15.4 Noise Nuisance and Antisocial Behaviour

In England & Wales there has, in recent years, been an overlap between antisocial behaviour and noise nuisance. This has arisen since the introduction of the Anti-social Behaviour, Crime and Policing Act 2014.

Where noise falls below the threshold that is required to meet the test of being a Statutory Nuisance, but where it can be shown that the noise is a) unreasonable, b) persistent and c) is having a detrimental impact on the locality, the local authority or housing association can consider issuing a community protection notice. It is worth noting antisocial behaviour need not just be caused by individuals, the legislation also covers commercial/business activities.

A written warning to the person committing the anti-social behaviour must take place before serving the notice. The warning letter must identify the anti-social behaviour and provide a reasonable timescale for compliance. Examples where action may be appropriate could include causing a disturbance to the local community by playing loud music or early morning deliveries. Where the behaviour persists, a notice may be issued and can require the person responsible to stop the activity (such as stop playing loud music) or to take reasonable steps to achieve a specified result.

In severe case closure of residential or business premises can be ordered where the local authority is satisfied that nuisance and disorder have occurred or are likely to occur.

Any victim of antisocial noise can demand a case review using the 'community trigger' where the relevant threshold is met. The threshold must be no more than three complaints of antisocial behaviour in the preceding six months, for example, complaints about three separate noisy parties. The case review must examine what has been done to investigate the victim's complaints and produce recommendations on further action.

16. Planning and Noise

Noise is a frequent consideration in planning applications and is a material planning consideration as it may have significant impacts from some developments. It is also included as a consideration in the National Planning Policy Framework of 2019. Noise from a site may be a reason for imposing planning conditions or in some cases refusing a planning application.

The assessment of a planning application in terms of noise impact is whether there is "detriment or loss of amenity" to nearby occupiers or residents. In broad terms this means is there potential for damage or loss (which includes annoyance) from the proposed development? "Loss of amenity", for example the effect of increased noise levels in a garden, can be a subjective assessment and may need explanation in a planning consultation response, but is generally held to be a tighter standard than a Statutory Noise Nuisance. Tests as to whether a planning application requires a planning condition or refusal are set out in the National Planning Policy Guidance (Planning Practice Guidance, Noise / Noise Policy Statement for England – see section 20).

The Planning Practice Guidance on noise refers to the effect of the noise on inhabitants of the area or a nearby noise sensitive location, such as a school or hospital ("Observed Effect Levels"). It is different to a Statutory Noise Nuisance, and is a tighter standard in terms of being able to impose conditions as it looks at the potential for more minor disturbance and annoyance (Lowest Observed Adverse Effect Level and Observed Adverse Effect Level) than the significant impact required for Statutory Noise Nuisance (see section 15).

It is sensible for all planning applications, other than those for very minor changes, to be screened for noise impacts. This is for new potential noise sources being constructed or generated <u>and</u> for new noise sensitive receptors being built close to existing noise generators. Following screening, if it appears that noise may be an issue, then a noise assessment should be carried out. The assessment may involve asking for details of the plant and machinery, location of noise generating activities on the site, days and hours of operation, any proposed noise mitigation measure and so forth. The potential for noise from deliveries or mobile sources should not be overlooked.

The developer or applicant may have appointed a noise consultant and a report may have been prepared and submitted. Any report should be assessed to check it has used appropriate methodology, takes account of local conditions, considered all potential sources, and has examined likely impacts on the most critical noise sensitive locations. Commonly a noise assessment may have been made using British Standard BS 4142, (see section 20) as this standard assesses likely adverse impacts from noise sources on residential locations. In the case of applications for mineral activities e.g. quarrying, minerals planning guidance may have been used to carry out an assessment.

Where noise is found likely to cause a, "loss or detriment to amenity" (an Observed Adverse Effect or Significant Observed Adverse Effect on the behaviour of nearby residents), planning permission can be refused (rarely) or conditions imposed (most commonly). Any planning conditions imposed must be necessary, relevant, precise, enforceable and reasonable and must not be so restrictive that they actually mean the development cannot occur (in which case permission should have been refused). They must also be within the power of the applicant, i.e. not impose conditions on a third party who is nothing to do with the application. There is a need to check that any planning conditions are complied with.

In the case of proposed new noise generating activities, the sources should always be dealt with to reduce levels. It is not usually appropriate or legal to impose restrictions at the receiver e.g. the resident of an existing private house, as it will not be possible to enforce planning conditions on anyone other than the applicant. Where a noise sensitive development is built close to an existing noise source, other than measures such as building a noise barrier or installing sound insulation, there is often little else that can be imposed on the new occupiers as it is unlikely it will be complied with or can be enforced; i.e. residents having a condition that they cannot use their gardens during the day because of the noise from the adjoining site. In addition, it is unlikely that the existing factory can have new planning controls placed on its operation if they are not the applicant. Furthermore, the National Planning Framework suggests that existing business should not have undue restrictions placed on them because of changes in nearby land use.

Occasionally a developer will try to impose a covenant or other legal restriction on a new development restricting their right to complain against the noise, and may use this as a way of achieving planning permission, (for example for a new house on a vacant plot of land next to a shooting range). Such a covenant is a civil matter between the parties, but it is highly unlikely that it would be accepted as valid by a Local Authority or court should the new resident decide to complain about the noise, as they have a Statutory right to complain under the Environmental Protection Act, and it would probably conflict with basic rights under the Human Rights Act. Therefore such agreements should not be accepted as a way of achieving planning permission where noise impact would suggest planning permission should be refused.

The issue of creeping intensification of the noise climate should be considered. This is where a series of developments occur, and each one does have an impact on noise levels, but not at a level that requires refusal or the imposition of planning conditions. As each application is dealt with individually, and each assess the noise climate at the time of application, and the background noise levels against which an assessment is made include the previous development, the noise levels are gradually allowed to increase. This can cause resentment from local residents, but is hard to deal with in planning terms, made harder because of guidance in the National Planning Policy Framework that existing business should not have undue restrictions placed on them because of changes in nearby land use since they were established. It can mean that planning conditions should not be imposed on developments by an existing business, just because other new businesses have resulted in increased noise levels in the locality.

Finally, it should be remembered that a planning permission can result in the change in the nature and character of an area, for example a new factory changes the area from a purely residential one to a mixed residential and industrial area. This can have significant ramifications in Statutory Noise Nuisance assessments, as noise nuisance relates to the nature and character of the area, which the planning application has changed. Thus a noise that would previously have been considered a Statutory Noise Nuisance in a solely residential area may now not be considered a Statutory Nuisance in a mixed use area.

In certain larger industrial premises the activities on the site are required to have a Permit to operate the activity because of its potential to pollute under the Pollution Prevention and Control Act 1999 and the Environmental Permitting Regulations 2016. Known as A1 and A2 Activities, the noise element of the activities will have been dealt with as part of the Permit application process following National Guidance (Horizontal Guidance H3: Environmental Permitting) though again this should be checked at the planning application stage.

Some developments, because of their scale, will have required an Environmental Impact Assessment (EIA). All the impacts and releases to the environment should have been assessed by the developer if an EIA has been required, and therefore detailed noise information should be available at the planning application stage for review. The data should include all the potential noise sources, likely impacts and mitigation measures proposed to minimise any adverse noise effects. It is still necessary to thoroughly check that all potential sources have been considered, impacts examined, mitigation measures scrutinised and sensitive receiver locations assessed.

17. Particular Sources of Environmental Noise

There are many sources and potential sources of noise, however complaints to Local Authorities are surveyed annually by the Chartered Institute of Environmental Health and Table 6 shows the most common from 2012/3 data.

It is interesting that noise perceived as unnecessary, such as loud music or barking dogs are more common causes of complaint than noise sources that are seen as necessary or good for society, even though they may be at a similar level, such as children playing, railway trains or aircraft. Certain sounds such as barking dogs are clearly designed through evolution to attract attention or act as a warning and can cause considerable distress as sufferers may find they tune into the noise and actively anticipate the next period of noise.

Industrial noise, unless it is particularly tonal or has some other particular characteristic, is not generally the subject of a great many noise complaints. Interestingly, natural sounds such as bird song, waves on a beach or wind in trees, though they can be relatively loud, do not generate the same level of disturbance or annoyance.

TABLE 6 SOURCES OF COMPLAINT TO ENVIRONMENTAL HEALTH DEPARTMENTS IN ENGLAND & WALES

1. Residential and domestic (barking dogs, loud music, TVs etc) 63%

2. Pubs Clubs & Restaurants 5%

3. Commercial (offices, shops, public transport) 4%

4. Vehicles machinery & equipment in the street 4%

5. Construction & demolition 3%

6. Leisure facilities (fairs, sports grounds etc) 2%

7. Industrial 1%

8. Agricultural >1%

   Other unspecified noise sources 16%

   (Figures do not equal 100% due to rounding)

18. Workplace Noise

Workplace noise is noise that occurs at the workplace, which can be indoors and outdoors. The main issue in relation to this noise is the risk of hearing damage and hearing loss due to high noise exposures. Noise above 80 dBA has the potential, if exposure is prolonged, to cause temporary and long term damage to hearing. If very loud, above 130 dBA, very short term noise exposure can cause permanent damage to hearing.

Short term effects can include "ringing in the ears" (tinnitus), and temporary deafness (sometimes called temporary threshold shift). If exposure is prolonged, the inner ear becomes damaged and permanent hearing loss (permanent threshold shift) and permanent tinnitus can occur. Sometimes other auditory damage can occur, also making sounds difficult to hear.

To control noise in the workplace, Regulations have been introduced under the Health and Safety at Work Act 1974, The Control of Noise at Work Regulations 2005. However, irrespective of the Legislation, sensible employers will minimise exposure to noise for both employees and other people who may be at the site.

18.1 Health and Safety at Work Act 1974

This Act has the purpose of "securing the health, safety and welfare of persons at work". It also protects people who are not at work from risks to their health and safety created or caused by the activities of persons at work. Everyone at work is covered by the Act, including the self employed, sub contractors and volunteers or interns.

http://www.legislation.gov.uk/ukpga/1974/37/contents

There are 4 sections that are of greatest importance in terms of noise:

Section 2 General Duties of Employers. The employer has to, as far as is reasonably practicable, ensure the health safety and welfare of his/her employees.

Section 3 General Duties of Employers to Other Persons. This section imposes a duty to persons who are not his/her employees, which can include members of the public, visitors, and contractors.

Section 4 General Duties of Persons concerned with Premises to Other Persons. This imposes a duty on the person having control of a premises to persons who are not their employees but use the premises as a place of work, for example contractors.

Section 7 General Duties of Employees. Employees have a duty to take reasonable care for their own health & safety and have a duty to co-operate with the employer so he/she can comply with their statutory duties.

In addition Section 8 imposes a duty on employers not to interfere with or misuse anything provided in the interests of health and safety, such as noise shielding round a machine or deliberately damaging any hearing protection provided. Section 9 imposes a duty on employers not to charge for anything provided as a requirement of the Act, for example hearing protection.

Enforcement of the Act is split between the Health and Safety Executive and Local Authorities, depending upon the industry, and can vary between informal cautions to Improvement Notices, requiring action to be taken (for example providing hearing protection), Prohibition Notices, prohibiting the activity or use of a piece of plant and machinery, and prosecution in the most serious breaches of the Act.

18.2 The Control of Noise at Work Regulations 2005

These Regulations impose limits and controls on the noise exposure of employees and the self employed at all workplaces and work activities (with some very limited exemptions for emergency services and the military). The basic thrust of the regulations is that noise exposure should be eliminated where possible or should be reduced to the lowest level as is reasonably practical (Regulation 6). Employers have to assess their workplaces and noise exposures of employees and where certain action levels or limits are exceeded carry out steps to reduce noise exposure, provide hearing protection, set up hearing protection zones or areas, and provide health surveillance.

http://www.legislation.gov.uk/uksi/2005/1643/contents/made

The Regulations have two Noise Exposure Action Levels and an Exposure Limit Value (see Table 7). The Noise Exposure Action Levels are the Upper Exposure Level and the Lower Exposure Level. These are based on a Daily Personal Exposure to Noise (Lep,d), (or a Weekly Personal Exposure to Noise (Lep,w)) and a peak sound pressure level (LCpeak). The Exposure Limit Value is also based on a daily personal exposure to noise (Lep,d) or weekly personal exposure to noise (Lep,w).

TABLE 7 CONTROL OF NOISE AT WORK REGULATIONS ACTION AND LIMIT VALUES

Lower Exposure Action Level	80dB A weighted (Lep,d) or (Lep,w)
	135dB C weighted Peak
Upper Exposure Action Level	85dB A weighted (Lep,d) or (Lep,w)
	137dB C weighted Peak
Exposure Limit Value	87dB A weighted (Lep,d) or (Lep,w)
	140dB C weighted Peak

So what does an employer need to do?

Where an employer carries out an activity that creates noise they must ask themselves whether the noise is likely to expose employees at a level that is equal to or above the Lower Exposure Action Level. To answer this question the employer must undertake a risk assessment of the noise, an assessment of working patterns and behaviours of those likely to be exposed to the noise, noise levels of machines and equipment and this may include noise level measurements. If the employer determines that employee's noise exposure is above an action level or the limit value, or is likely to be above, then they are required to take steps.

It is important for the employer to consider both parameters, the daily or weekly personal noise exposure (Lep,d or Lep,w) **and** the Peak sound pressure levels LCpeak. As a guide, the Peak sound pressure level should be measured whenever there is exposure to short term impact noise, such as might occur from a metal press or riveting.

Noise exposure above the Exposure Limit Value

The employer must takes steps to ensure that employees noise exposure is reduced to below the Exposure Limit Value by reducing noise from the source (noise insulation for example) and by the use of suitable hearing protection and other appropriate measures. An employee's noise exposure must not exceed the Exposure Limit Value but in assessing this, the effect of any hearing protection being worn by the employee should be taken into account.

Noise exposure at or above the Upper Exposure Action Level.

The employer must take measures to reduce the noise exposure, primarily by reducing the noise from the source or by removing the need for the employee to be close to the noise source. If this cannot be achieved they must ensure that suitable hearing protection is provided and that its use is compulsory in "Hearing Protection Zones", areas where access should be prohibited for those without adequate hearing protection. The employer must also arrange for health surveillance (hearing checks) for employees likely to be exposed above the Upper Exposure Action Level. In assessing compliance against this Action level, the effect of any hearing protection being won by the employee should not be taken into account.

Noise exposure at or above the Lower Exposure Action Level

The employer must take steps to reduce noise exposure and provide information and training on noise exposure to employees. Hearing protection must be available on request to employees and employees trained how to use and maintain it.

Noise exposure below the Lower Exposure Action Level

An employer who has assessed noise exposures and found they are below the Lower Exposure Action Level does not need to provide any hearing protection, health screening signage or other hearing protection measures. There remains a duty to comply with the regulations and so should working patterns change, new plant and machinery be installed or alterations to the workplace or plant and machinery take place, employers should look at reassessing the situation to see if a new risk assessment is necessary. In addition if complaints or comments from employees regarding noise occur, this should be taken as a sign to reassess the situation. There is also the general duty in the Regulations to reduce noise levels as low as is reasonably practicable.

What is Daily or Weekly Personal Exposure to Noise (Lep,d or Lep,w)?

Daily or weekly personal exposure to noise is a sound index which provides a single value noise level based on the A weighted sound pressure levels that an employee is exposed to over a working day or week and the duration of exposure. It can be thought of as their daily "noise dose". The intention of having a single figure is that many workers noise exposures vary during a working day depending on their job, the plant and equipment in use, which may vary during the day, and they may have differing working hours on different days. Using a daily or weekly index which takes account of this allows their actual noise exposure to be assessed against a standard designed to protect against hearing damage. Normally assessing a workers daily exposure is sufficient, but where an employee has a very varied job and their noise exposure may vary considerably, not just during the day but from day to day, then a weekly noise exposure figure may be a more suitable.

How do we work out Lep,d or Lep,w ?

Lep,d relates to the duration of the employees working day and the noise levels they are exposed to (LAeq) against a reference 8 hour period. For example, if they are exposed to a continuous noise level of 90 dBA for 8 hours then their daily personal noise exposure will be 90 dBA Lep,d. In practice of course employees will take breaks, work on differing machines and processes, work longer or shorter days, and machines will produce different noise levels at different times and thus it is necessary to calculate all the different noise levels and periods to compare against the reference period.

Some sound level meters and noise dosimeters will calculate Lep,d directly, however with others it may be necessary to calculate the noise exposure from measurements that have been made. The noise measurements at an employee's workplace should be A weighted and made using Leq's (equivalent continuous sound levels). All the locations where the employee works should be measured and results recorded. It important to know the durations of different noise exposure periods at each of the locations as well as the noise levels and from this information Lep,d can be calculated. The simplest way is to use a noise exposure calculator and there are a range of noise calculators available online to carry out these calculations including:

http://www.hse.gov.uk/noise/calculator.htm

https://www.noisemeters.co.uk/apps/naw/help/lepd-calculator.asp

http://www.xpglobe.com/bbc/noise/calc/

If you want to work out the calculation yourself then the following equation should be used (for a simple noise level such as 85 dB LAeq over 6 hours):

Lep,d = LAeq, *Te* + 10Log$_{10}$ (*Te*/*T0*)

Where:

Te is the duration of the person's working day, in seconds

T0 is the 8 hour reference period in seconds (i.e. 28,800 seconds)

For example

6 hours (21600 seconds) of noise exposure at 80 dB LAeq

Lep,d = 80dB (21600 seconds) + 10log(21600/28800)

Lep,d = 80dB (21600 seconds) + 10log(0.75)

Lep,d = 80dB (21600 seconds) +10 x -0.12

Lep,d = 80dB (21600 seconds) -1.2

Lep,d = 80 – 1.2 = 78.8 Lep,d

For more complex patterns of work the following equation should be used, but to avoid error one of the readily available online noise calculators is recommended.

Lep,d =10log$_{10}$($\frac{1}{T0} \sum_{i=1}^{n} Ti10^{0.1(LAeq,T)i}$**)**

Where:

T0 = 28800 seconds

Ti = duration of period in seconds

n = number of periods in the day

(LAeq ,T)i = LAeq representing the persons noise exposure during period i

19. Hearing Protection

The best form of hearing protection is to avoid exposure to the high levels of noise! This is best achieved by reducing the noise at source — such as by installing a quieter machine. If this is not possible, then the next best method is to prevent exposure by preventing access to noisy areas, such as enclosures around machines, or placing noisy plant in areas which are not easily accessed, such as in dedicated plant rooms, and ensuring access by people is prohibited. Only if noise levels cannot be reduced at source, or access to noisy areas is unavoidable, should hearing protection be used as a method of reducing exposure.

Hearing protection should never be the first resort in reducing noise exposure, and should be needed only where the exposure reduction methods have failed or cannot be used. This is because they put the onus on the employee to protect their own hearing rather than it being the employer's responsibility. In addition, it is easy to get it wrong with hearing protection, to fit ear plugs incorrectly, to select the wrong type of hearing protection, to misuse it and damage it so that it is less effective. Unless hearing protection is rigorously enforced by management it is often easily avoided, either deliberately or by accident (the worker temporarily working in a noisy area when he/she does not normally).

Hearing protection areas must be clearly identified with clear signs, which meet legislative requirements. Staff must be trained in the correct use of hearing protection, it is not good enough for employers to issue hearing protection without training. The equipment must also be suitable for the particular situation. Different types of hearing protection provide differing levels of protection; some are suitable with safety glasses and visors, other are not for example. The hearing protection should be inspected regularly for damage and replaced periodically. They should be individually allocated, not shared between employees. Finally, spare hearing protection should be easily available; (for example at the entrance to a noisy area), for employees or contractors who, while not working in that area, may occasionally have need to enter it.

To select appropriate hearing protection the employer will have needed to carry out a workplace noise assessment. This should have identified, under The Control of Noise at Work Regulations, where hearing protection is advised and where its use is essential. Where hearing protection is shown by the assessment as required, the noise levels should be further measured to assess the noise in the locations where workers are exposed. The measurements for determining suitable hearing protection should include peak noise levels (C weighted), Octave Bands, and C weighted Leq as well as LAeq.

These results can then be compared with the performance of differing types of hearing protection available, using one of 3 differing techniques (Octave Band, HML (High Medium and Low) or SNR (Single number rating)) so that those which provide adequate noise reduction at the ear, and are most suitable in terms of comfort and wearability, can be chosen. The manufacturers of hearing protection will be able to provide data sheets on the noise reduction properties of their hearing protection, and may be willing to provide samples so that comfort and wearability can be assessed. Details on comparing the performance of hearing protection and assessing the correct one can be obtained from HSE document "Controlling Noise at Work The Control of Noise at Work Regulations 2005 – Guidance on Regulations – L108"

http://www.hse.gov.uk/pubns/priced/l108.pdf

There is also an online hearing protection calculator available from the HSE which provides a simple way of selecting suitable hearing protection providing that noise exposures are known and manufacturer's data is available. It may not be suitable for all circumstances and if any doubt exists expert advice should be sought.

http://www.hse.gov.uk/noise/calculator.htm

20. Some Commonly Used Noise Standards and Guidance

There are a range of noise standards and guidance that have been published and may need to be complied with when investigating or assessing noise. Some of the most common are briefly described below:

BS4142:2014 Method for Rating Industrial and Commercial Sound

This British Standard provides a methodology of assessing noise that affects residential properties or predicting the effect of a new noise source likely to affect a residential property, against the likelihood of complaints occurring. It is widely used in planning applications and sometimes in assessing the validity of complaints about commercial and industrial noise. The most recent version from 2014 has been updated in 2019. The introduction to the standard makes it clear that the standard is not for the determination of noise nuisance, or for non industrial or commercial noise sources.

The standard works on the basis of comparing the specific noise source of interest (i.e. a particular fan, machine etc) with the background noise level (L90) after the application of correction factors for ambient noise, intermittency, tonal characteristics, time of day etc to provide an indication of the significance of the impact of the noise under investigation (the specific noise).

http://shop.bsigroup.com/ProductDetail/?pid=000000000030268408

BS 5228 Code of Practice for Noise and Vibration Control on Construction and Open Sites

This British Standard provides information on methods of noise and vibration control on construction and demolition sites as well as other sources such as mineral extraction (open cast coal etc). It covers sources of noise and potential impacts on workers, the community and the nearby environment.

Information is provided on screening and barriers to control noise, and what can be particularly useful in determining noise from new or planned activities, typical noise levels from a range of plant, equipment and activities, such as dumper trucks, excavators, cutting concrete etc. This is an "Approved Cope of Practice" under the Control of Pollution Act 1974 meaning that in the case of construction and demolition sites the approaches outlined to minimise noise can be enforced in certain circumstances.

BS5228 can be particularly useful in predicting and noise levels from proposed activities at the planning consent stage, when on site noise level measurements are not available. The current version dates from 2009, amended in 2014. A new updated version is expected in the near future.

https://shop.bsigroup.com/ProductDetail?pid=000000000030258086

Minerals Policy Statement 2 Controlling and mitigating the environmental effects of mineral extraction in England (Annex 2 - Noise) 2005

This document form planning guidance and criteria concerning noise from mineral extraction processes such as quarries. It is aimed at planning applications and new mineral extraction developments. The document provides guidance on factors concerning noise and the proposed operations that should be considered as well as maximum noise levels which should not be exceeded at nearby residential properties, with different levels for day, evening and night-time. It also sets a limit based on background noise levels and provides an allowance for short term activities where noise levels may be greater. It suggests how monitoring of noise should be undertaken, and in the Appendices provides some example of good practice ion noise control. The document is currently archived in the National Archives.

http://webarchive.nationalarchives.gov.uk/20120919132719/http://www.communities.gov.uk/documents/planningandbuilding/pdf/mps2annex2.pdf

Planning Practice Guidance, Noise / Noise Policy Statement for England

This guidance issued under the National Planning Policy Framework sets out when noise is relevant to planning, i.e. should be taken into account in planning applications. Three guidance levels are given, known as "Observed Effect Levels", varying between No Observed Effect Level, Lowest Observed Adverse Effect Level and Significant Observed Adverse Effect Level (Observed Adverse Effect and Unacceptable Adverse Effect). These are based on changes in behaviour that are likely to result at differing noise levels in varying circumstances. Actual noise levels are not stated, but examples of the differing behaviours are given, and guidance on what steps are required in planning terms, ranging from no action, to prevent from occurring and avoid for Unacceptable Adverse effect levels.

The aims of the guidance are:

> 1 that significant adverse effects on health and quality of life should be avoided,

> 2 that adverse effects on health and quality of life from noise should be minimised and mitigated,

> 3 where possible improve health and quality of life by managing and mitigating noise.

https://www.gov.uk/guidance/noise--2

https://www.gov.uk/government/uploads/system/uploads/attachment_data/file/69533/pb13750-noise-policy.pdf

Horizontal Guidance H3: Environmental Permitting

This guidance document is in two parts and is intended to provide guidance on noise from "Permitted" or "Regulated" activities (those that require a permit to operate under the Pollution Prevention and Control (England & Wales) Regulations 2016). Part 1 sets out the broad regulatory framework under which Permits will be issued and conditions set for operators, whilst Part 2 is the more technical guidance on noise measurement, prediction and assessment, to show compliance with permit noise conditions and best practice. It also has some very useful sections on basic principles of acoustics, sound attenuation and sound measurement.

This guidance is applicable to those which are classified as "A1" or "A2 Regulated" activities (where all emissions to air, water and land are regulated). "A1" activities are regulated by the Environment Agency and "A2" by Local Authorities. The guidance may therefore be used by both regulatory agencies. There is an overarching principle that noise levels from an "A1" or "A2" Regulated activity should not be loud enough to give reasonable cause of annoyance to persons in the vicinity or beyond the installation boundary (a tighter standard than Statutory Noise Nuisance).

The guidance is available from **https://www.gov.uk/government/collections/ horizontal-guidance-environmental-permitting**

Neighbourhood Noise Policies and Practice for Local Authorities – A Management Guide

This detailed guidance document was published by Defra and the Chartered Institute of Environmental Health in 2006. It is now out of date as legislation and some standards have moved on; however it provides a useful summary of nuisance law, the responsibilities of Local Authorities, advice on how Local Authority services might be structured, and how complaints and enquiries regarding noise may best be addressed. There are a series of practice guides and checklists, including: investigating complaints, formal interviews, witness statements, dealing with persons with mental illness etc, and these can be very helpful.

The document is no longer available for download from the CIEH website, but may be available by an internet search.

Guidelines for Community Noise 1999 WHO

This very detailed and comprehensive guidance from the World Health Organisation examines many sources of noise and noise exposure, particularly in relation to effects on health. In Chapter 4 it suggests some noise levels which are considered appropriate to protect against noise in a variety of scenarios, from hearing impairment to speech interference, and annoyance to sleep disturbance, in domestic dwellings and other noise sensitive locations such as hospitals and schools. These guideline values can be useful in considering health effects of noise in relation to Statutory Nuisance, in planning applications and new developments.

The guidance examines noise management strategies and concludes with suggestions for government, both local and national on noise reduction and control.

http://www.who.int/en/

BS8233:1999 Sound Insulation & Noise Reduction for Buildings

This British Standard provides information on noise within buildings and the design of buildings to control noise from plant and machinery within the building as well as from external sources and differing uses within the same building. It has internal noise criteria for various types of use, such as classrooms, staff rooms, offices, canteens, but also includes residential living rooms and bedrooms.

The Building Regulations 2010 Resistance to the Passage of Sound, Approved document E

This document provides a wealth of information on construction techniques that, if carried out competently, should meet the sound insulation requirements of the Building Regulations in relation to schools, new residential buildings and conversions to residential uses of existing buildings. It sets out performance standards in respect of insulation, and then provides details, including diagrams of how this can be achieved by differing construction techniques and materials, covering walls, floors ceilings, joints and junctions. It is available from the Governments Planning Portal website https://www.planningportal.co.uk/info/200135/approved_documents/67/part_e_-_resistance_to_the_passage_of_sound

21. Carrying Out an Environmental Noise Assessment

1. The first step in an environmental noise assessment is to find out exactly what you are measuring and why. Is it environmental noise from a factory affecting neighbouring houses causing complaint, or is it for planning purposes?

2. The next stage is to find out some background information to give you an understanding of the issues or problems you might encounter when making any measurements, and where measurements are best made. Don't skimp on this stage, the more information that can be gathered here the better and easier your measurements will be. This information includes:

    2.1. Understanding what the site or business actually does, such as what do they make and using what machines?

    2.2. What are the hours of operation of the activity, or working day?

2.3. What standards, legislation or local controls, such as planning conditions, codes of practice or company procedures/limits apply?

2.4. Are there any previous noise surveys or studies that may be relevant or that would be worth repeating?

2.5. Is there a history of concerns or complaints about any noise on or from the site, and if so what are the specific details of this?

2.6. Who is requiring the noise measurements, the company to establish noise levels inside or outside the site, a Local Authority to assess compliance with planning conditions, for a planning application for a new development, or a regulator in respect of noise disturbance to nearby residents?

3. Now you need to plan your noise measurement exercise, again this is a stage that is worth spending time on to be able to make the most effective and appropriate measurements.

3.1. Do you have a suitable Sound Level Meter that can actually do what you want? Is it suitable for environmental noise, does it have a suitable battery life or is it mains powered, is it portable or meant to be fixed. Do you have a suitable "field calibrator" and do the sound level meter and calibrator have in date service and calibration certificates?

3.2. Do you want to record the noise as audio so you can listen to it again or even process it in some way after the recording to gain additional information? (Many sound level meters can record sound, some for short periods, some for many hours)

3.3. Does the sound level meter actually meet the requirements of any standard, code of practice or legislation that applies or you want to use?

3.4. Do you have and will you need wind or rain shields? If you are proposing to use them do you have information on the effects of them on noise levels? (There might be a slight reduction in measured levels).

3.5. Do you want to take photographs of the site, noise source under investigation, layout, monitoring location etc? Photographs can be a very useful record of conditions at the time of measurement, but permission may be required beforehand in order to do this.

3.6. Do you have maps or plans of the site or area, or proposed location for new developments? These can be useful for identifying monitoring locations and noise sources both before and during measurement.

3.7. Do you know where you actually want to make your noise level measurements, have you sorted out if access is possible or allowed?

3.8. What times of day or night are you going to make measurements? When is the factory floor busiest, when do shut down periods occur, e.g. lunch breaks etc?

3.9. Health and safety, do you need safety boots, safety glasses, hearing protection or specialist clothing (e.g. flameproof boiler suits etc) to access the factory floor, will you need outdoor all weather clothing?

4. Now make your measurements in line with your plan. This again is a multi stage process and remember that although your results can and may be challenged or subject to dispute, detailed records you make at the time should be a true reflection of what you observed and therefore cannot easily be challenged, particularly if the challenger was not present at the time of the measurements.

4.1. Make a note of how the instrument is set up, frequency weightings used, averaging periods, height of microphone, if a microphone extension cable and tripod is used.

4.2. Calibrate you instruments using your "field calibrator" and record that you have done so.

4.3. Note the weather conditions, temperature, wind direction, estimate of wind speed etc

4.4. Make detailed notes on your measurement location(s) distance from walls and structures, estimate of height, can you see the noise source or specific machine? Note machine serial numbers or plant reference numbers in a factory.

4.5. Note any other noise sources or factors that might influence any measurements, such as other machines, traffic noise, barking dogs, effects of noise reflective surfaces, any barriers, the type of ground or surface over which the sound passes etc. It is always useful to "paint a picture" of the environment in which you are measuring, at the time of the measurements, as this puts any measurements in context, and you can always refer to this later.

4.6. Note anything that might be unusual for the factory or area, such as low flying aircraft, nearby building works, a particular machine in a factory not working when it does normally.

4.7. Make a note of any assumptions you have made; such as the machines are operating normally, that all plant is in use at the time of measurement.

4.8. Make your measurements.

4.9. Note anything that changes during the measurements.

4.10. After completing the measurements calibrate the sound level meter(s) again and record that you have done so.

5. Finally review and process your data, and write up your results. Include in your report details from the notes you made, maps and plans, assumptions you made etc.

22. Carrying Out an Occupational Noise Assessment

1. The first step in any occupational noise monitoring exercise, is to find out exactly what you are measuring and why. Is it noise in a factory which may damage hearing for example and just a routine survey, or is it in relation to complaints or concerns from employees. Is it to assess effectiveness of workplace hearing protection control such as hearing protection usage?

2. The next stage is to find out some background information to give you an understanding of the issues or problems you might encounter when making any measurements, and where measurements are best made. Don't skimp on this stage, the more information that can be gathered here the better and easier your measurements will be. This information includes:

    2.1. Understanding what the site or business actually does, such as what do they make and using which machines.

    2.2. What are the hours of operation of the activity, or working day?

    2.3. What standards, legislation, company procedures/limits apply? The most important are likely to be The Control of Noise at Work Regulations.

    2.4. Are there any previous noise surveys or studies that may be relevant or that would be worth repeating?

    2.5. Is there a history of concerns or complaints about any noise on or from the site, and if so what are the specific details of this?

    2.6. Who is requiring the noise measurement: a regulator in respect of occupational noise exposure, the company to assess noise levels on the site and the need for hearing protection, workers in a particular area worried about their noise exposure?

3. Now you need to plan your noise measurement exercise, again this is a stage that is worth spending time on to be able to make the most effective and appropriate measurements.

3.1. Do you have a suitable sound level meter that can actually do what you want? Is it suitable for occupational noise level assessments, can it calculate Lep,d, does it have a suitable battery life, is it portable. Do you have a suitable "field calibrator" and do the sound level meter and calibrator have in date service and calibration certificates.

3.2. Do you want to record the noise as audio so you can listen to it again or even process it in some way after the recording to gain additional information? (Many sound level meters can record sound, some for short periods, some for many hours).

3.3. Do you want to use noise dosimeters to actually measure the noise exposure of individual employees: how many will you need, how will you determine which employees are chosen to wear them, how will you check that employees don't tamper with them to artificially raise or lower recorded noise exposure?

3.4. Does the sound level meter or dosimeter actually meet the requirements of any standard, code of practice or legislation that applies or you want to use?

3.5. Do you want to take photographs of the site, noise source under investigation, layout, monitoring location etc? Photographs can be a very useful record of conditions at the time of measurement, but permission may be required beforehand in order to do this.

3.6. Do you have maps or plans of the site or factory floor showing individual plant and machinery? These can be useful for identifying monitoring locations and noise sources both before and during measurement.

3.7. Are you clear on employees working patterns and jobs, do you know all of the noise sources that will need to be assessed to work out what noise sources they are exposed to over a typical day or week?

3.8. Do you know where you actually want to make your noise level measurements, have you sorted out if access is possible or allowed?

3.9. What times of day or night are you going to make measurements? When is the factory floor busiest, when do shut down periods occur, e.g. lunch breaks etc?

3.10. Health and safety, do you need safety boots, safety glasses, hearing protection or specialist clothing (e.g. flameproof boiler suits etc) to access the factory floor, will you need outdoor all weather clothing?

4. Now make your measurements in line with your plan. This again is a multi stage process and remember that although your results can and may be challenged or subject to dispute, any detailed records you make at the time should be a true

reflection of what you observed and therefore cannot easily be challenged, particularly if the challenger was not present at the time of the measurements.

4.1. Make a note of how the instrument is set up, frequency weightings used, averaging periods, height of microphone, if a microphone extension cable and tripod is used.

4.2. Calibrate you instruments using your "field calibrator" and record that you have done so.

4.3. Note the conditions in the factory, does all the plant appear to be in use, are some machines not working. Ask **employees,** if possible, if the site is operating normally and if they are doing their normal roles, some plant may have been switched off to reduce noise levels etc.

4.4. Make detailed notes on your measurement location(s), distance from walls and structures, what are the internal surfaces, hard reflective like concrete or soft absorbent ones? Estimate of height of the workplace. Is this where an employee actually works? Machine serial numbers or reference numbers in a factory.

4.5. When making measurements be aware of the microphone location. Measurements are meant to be made in an undisturbed field, i.e. at the head height of the operator, but without the operator present, to avoid reflections from the body. If the measurements can only be made with the operator present try and pick a representative location, but at least 4 cm from the operators head. Not too close to the source, but not so far away that reflections from other surfaces may result in increased noise levels.

4.6. Note any other noise sources or factors that might influence any measurements, such as other machines, external noise such as traffic noise, radios on site. It is always useful to "paint a picture" of the environment in which you are measuring, at the time of the measurements, as this puts any measurements in context, and you can always refer to this later.

4.7. Note anything that might be unusual for the factory or area, such as low flying aircraft, nearby building works, a particular machine in a factory not working when it does normally.

4.8. Make a note of any assumptions you have made, such as that the machines are operating normally, that all plant is in use at the time of measurement.

4.9. Make your measurements.

4.10. Note anything that changes during the measurements.

4.11. Check that employees are wearing hearing protection in hearing protection areas, see if you can examine the hearing protection in use to see what is being provided and if it is maintained.

4.12. After completing the measurements calibrate the sound level meter(s) again and record that you have done this.

5. Finally review and process your data, work out daily personal noise exposures, and write up your results. Include in your report details from the notes you made, maps and plans, assumptions you made etc.

23. Carrying Out a Noise Nuisance Assessment

A noise nuisance assessment is very different to other types of noise assessment. The most important being that there is, in the vast majority of cases, no requirement to carry out measurements using sound level meters. Only in the case of the 1996 Noise Act, (night time noise assessments within residential properties) are measurements necessary, and even then not in every instance. The main purposes for carrying out sound level measurements in noise nuisance assessments are three fold:

1) To confirm a Local Authorities officer opinion that a noise nuisance is occurring.

2) To provide additional data on the noise that is alleged to be a nuisance; tones, times of day, comparison with other noise sources etc.

3) To provide additional evidence that can be used in court

The assessment of noise nuisance is an assessment by a suitably qualified, experienced and properly authorised officer of a Local Authority on how a noise is impacting on a person or group of residents rights over and enjoyment of land. The assessment is based upon factors including the source of the noise, the necessity for the noise, the impact the noise is having on the recipient and how it is affecting them, the nature and character of the area. Noise level measurements cannot replace these subjective assessments, but can help to influence an officer's opinion in terms of identifying tones, how loud it is compared to other noise sources, when it occurs, how often it occurs.

Some experienced Local Authority officers prefer not to use sound level meters and noise monitoring equipment in assessing noise nuisance, as it can be a distraction in determining nuisance. Discussion, particularly if a case should go to court, becomes focused on technical issues around the instrumentation, rather than the most important factor, whether the noise is an unreasonable interference. This will be a case by case decision based on the source of the noise, experience of the officer and policy of the Local Authority.

There are particular benefits in carrying out sound level measurements in the case of commercial or industrial noise sources, such as:

➢ Allowing comparison with background noise levels and other criteria, such as sleep disturbance.

➢ Identifying particular sources on busy industrial sites.

➢ Identifying any particular tones or other factors that may make a sound particularly noticeable, disturbing or annoying.

➢ Enabling the assessment of trends over time, allowing the effectiveness of any measures taken to reduce noise levels to be assessed.

If noise monitoring using instrumentation is to be carried out, then the process is very similar to an environmental noise assessment (See Section 21).

23.1 Noise Nuisance Recorders

Noise nuisance recorders have been in use for a number of years by many Local Authorities and others such as Housing Associations. They usually consist of a briefcase or similar container inside of which is noise monitoring and recording equipment that can be left at a complainant's property. This enables the resident to record noise when it affects them. Noise nuisance recorders can be particularly useful for intermittent noise, noise which is unpredictable in nature, for allowing residents to record noise that is actually affecting them, and for providing evidence. They can also be useful for identifying patterns in noise, such as a particular machine that switches on and off, and can even provide frequency analysis of the noise which can be very useful in industrial noise situations, for example identifying the noise making machine/fan etc.

Most noise nuisance recorders consist of a sound level meter which is situated in a locked container or case and measures noise levels via an external microphone. It also has the ability to record audio when a control button is pressed. Noise levels are usually measured continuously, but audio recordings only occur when activated by the resident, though some systems have pre triggers that record sound before the audio recording is actually operated, and sometimes post triggers which mean that the recording continues after the trigger is switched off. These can be useful for short term noise such as dogs barking where by the time the resident has operated the record switch the noise has ceased (particularly useful where noise occurs late at night).

Data gather is usually downloaded in the office when the equipment has been collected from the resident's property, although some systems now have remote access via the mobile phone network.

These systems are usually designed to be installed unobtrusively and to be battery and mains powered so can be installed in whichever room the resident feels they are most bothered by noise. Care has to be taken with them as although measured noise levels are not an issue, the audio recording will record private information from within the residents own property, but also potentially from neighbouring properties, (such as telephone calls, conversations etc). Residents who have these installed in their properties must be made aware of this to avoid future embarrassment or revealing of private data. The possibility of obtaining private data should mean the provisions of the Regulatory Investigatory Powers Act should also be considered before they are used.

If noise nuisance recorders are to be used the possibility of them being tampered with should always be kept in mind, either deliberately (such as hanging the microphone out of the window or the resident playing previously recorded noise to increase noise levels artificially) or accidentally. They should be used with noise log or diary sheets as well, because although useful in any subsequent hearing, they do not actually show the full impact or distress of a noise source on a resident.

Often noise nuisance recorders are used in the initial investigation of noise complaints and to provide supporting evidence in cases. Occasionally the data from noise nuisance recorders alone is used to justify the service of an abatement notice. Due to the possibility of tampering, and the need to be able to provide a Local Authority officers opinion to a court if necessary, it is most common that they are used with evidence from visits by suitably qualified and authorised officers when the noise nuisance recorder data is used as supporting evidence, often of the scale, frequency of occurrence and impact of the noise on the resident.

23.2 Noise Apps

Noise Apps are a relatively new development in assessing noise nuisance. They allow a person being affected by noise to record the noise on their mobile phone or tablet and send it, with a commentary if necessary, to their Local Authority or Housing Association.

The user simply downloads the app to their device and when affected by the noise of concern record short samples of it on their device. The data is stored on the device in an encrypted format and a GPS record can be included which enables the user to record where the noise recording was made. Some systems allow the user to rate the noise that has been recorded using a simple scoring system. The data is then uploaded to the office dealing with the complaint for analysis.

It is anticipated that the Noise App, and similar tools that may be developed, may supersede the noise nuisance recorders. They may be particularly useful in the early stages of a noise complaint, avoiding the need to install a noise nuisance recorder, which are often limited in availability. As with noise nuisance recorders there is always the potential of tampering with the noise levels to be considered, the issues of recording private information may be significant, and it is still be necessary for diary sheets or noise log sheets, or other evidence to be obtained to show the impact of the noise.

As this is a new product it is not yet clear how they will be used in practice and how the courts may assess the information gathered. It is recommended that they are used in the same way as a noise nuisance recorder, as an initial investigation tool and very useful supporting evidence when combined with a Local Authority officers opinion.

23.3 The Grim RIPA (the Regulation of Investigatory Powers Act 2000) and Surveillance Issues

Many noise nuisance cases involve assessing the noise created by one resident affecting an adjoining resident or residents (loud music, shouting etc). As such, when monitoring, gathering evidence and assessing the noise it must be borne in mind that this sort of noise nuisance investigation **is** surveillance of a resident or household and there are rules over what is allowed and how you go about it. If the rules are disregarded then the evidence that is gathered could be ruled inadmissible to a court and a case lost.

Information that is gathered must be made available to any defence and could potentially be examined in a court. This might include audio recordings (such as from a noise nuisance recorder) that contains private information, such as telephone or other conversations, arguments, names, dates and times of visitors. Such private information may be from the noise maker, but may also inadvertently be collected by the resident making the recordings, who will not be best pleased to have it made available to the defence or played in open court. It may also be breach of Article 8 of the Human Rights Act 1998.

It is recommended that any public authority involved in noise nuisance investigations should have clear procedures on carrying out monitoring, and these should be followed. The procedures should take account of the Human Rights Act and Regulation of Investigatory Powers Act 2000, and legal advice may be necessary to draw up such procedures. Some basic pointers are set out below, but you must satisfy yourself that you are following any procedures that are laid down and that these are up to date, as the legislation and legal opinion around this issue changes from time to time. (See Equalities & Human Rights Commission). **https://www.equalityhumanrights.com/en/ advice-and-guidance-human-rights-multipage-guide/right-respect-private-and-family-life-home-and**

The Grim RIPA – some basic points

- Listening to a person or recording a person amounts to surveillance under the Act.

- Authorisation is needed from a Justice of the Peace when surveillance is "directed surveillance".

- Surveillance is "directed surveillance" if it is covert, for a specific investigation and is likely to obtain or record private information.

- Covert means it is undertaken in a way that is calculated to ensure that persons who are subject to it are unaware of it.

- Intrusive surveillance is not permitted by Local Authorities. It involves the use of devices within a premises i.e. bugging a property.

- It is not an offence not to comply with the RIPA requirements, but it means data obtained may be ruled inadmissible in court.

- While it may be desirable in a nuisance case to carry out noise monitoring unobtrusively, this may fall under directed surveillance, being covert, for a specific investigation and possibly obtaining private information, requiring authorisation.

- Many Local Authorities as a matter of routine and courtesy notify those subject to nuisance complaints and inform them that noise monitoring (including noise recordings) may take place. This means that the surveillance is not covert.

- Where covert surveillance is proposed an order from a Justice of the Peace is required permitting the surveillance.

For more details see https://www.gov.uk/surveillance-and-counter-terrorism

24. Professional Bodies with Expertise and Sources of Information on Noise

There are a range of bodies with expertise in noise, noise law and noise measurement, the following provides a short description of some of them and the areas they cover.

Association of Noise Consultants

The Association of Noise Consultants is a trade association of over 100 noise, vibration and acoustics consultancies. It is possible to use the search facility on their website to find consultants in particular geographic areas or in specific areas of expertise.

http://www.association-of-noise-consultants.co.uk/

Chartered Institute of Environmental Health (CIEH)

The CIEH is a professional body made up of and representing Environmental Health Practitioners. It also campaigns on Environmental, Public Health and Occupational Health issues including noise. Most Local Authority Environmental Health Practitioners responsible for dealing with noise in planning applications, in the workplace or noise nuisances will be members. The CIEH carries out an annual survey of complaints to and actions taken by Local Authorities on noise, undertakes noise training, and have a range of guidance and publications.

http://www.cieh.org/

Environment Agency/Natural Resources Wales

The Environment Agency is an environmental regulator for England (Natural Resources Wales being their Welsh equivalent) with responsibility for a range of industries and emissions from them, including noise. Waste disposal and treatment sites, quarries, mines and many large industrial sites are regulated by them. They will issue Permits and consents for the operation of such sites, inspect and regulate them and will carry out monitoring at the sites they are responsible for, if necessary. They publish guidance on noise control at their Regulated or Permitted sites, including a specific guidance document for site operators and regulators known as "H3 Noise Assessment and Control".

https://www.gov.uk/government/organisations/environment-agency

https://www.gov.uk/government/collections/horizontal-guidance-environmental-permitting#h3-noise-assessment-and-control

Environment Law.org

This website is put together by the UK Environmental Law Association to provide basic legal information on a range of environmental issues. It includes a useful section on noise and refers to some interesting legal cases concerning environmental noise. It has links to and brief explanations of some of the most important and frequently used legislation covering noise.

http://www.environmentlaw.org.uk/rte.asp?id=31

Environmental Protection UK (EPUK)

EPUK (formerly the National Society for Clean Air) is a charity that campaigns, undertakes research and provides information on a wide range of environmental issues, including noise. It has a range of documents, guidance and leaflets. Most of the information is, at the present time, restricted to members of EPUK.

http://www.environmental-protection.org.uk/

Health & Safety Executive

The Health & Safety Executive is a regulator of many commercial and industrial activities for Health and Safety. They also carry out research and issue guidance and advice on health and safety matters including noise. Information available from them includes advice on hearing protection, Noise at Work Regulations, as well as guidance and information on certain industry sectors, for example noise in the entertainment sector.

http://www.hse.gov.uk/noise/index.htm

Institute of Acoustics

The Institute of Acoustics is a professional body for specialists in noise, acoustics and vibration. It has a journal, organises events and seminars, and produces guidance and technical papers on a range of noise related matters. It also has a range of noise courses and training events, responds to consultations and has specialist interest groups, including on Environmental Noise, Speech and Hearing and Noise & Vibration Engineering.

http://www.ioa.org.uk/

Institute of Sound & Vibration Research (ISVR)

ISVR, based at the University of Southampton, is an internationally recognised long standing research and consultancy centre in acoustics and vibration. As well as carrying out academic research it also has a commercial consulting arm. There are a large number of reports and papers published on its website, both from the main department and ISVR Consultancy services (the commercial consultancy arm) many of which provide useful information on specific topics.

http://www.southampton.ac.uk/engineering/research/centres/isvr.page

http://www.isvr.co.uk/index.htm

Institution of Occupational Safety & Health (IOSH)

The Institution of Occupational Safety & Health is a large worldwide body for Health & Safety Professionals. It has a range of guidance available and holds seminars and events on a wide range of workplace health and safety topics. Although covering many more workplace issues than noise it does have resources and guidance on noise in the workplace.

http://www.iosh.co.uk/About-us/Who-we-are.aspx

Noise Nuisance.org

This site, which is run by volunteer Environmental Health Professionals, provides some basic advice and guidance on noise nuisance. It is primarily aimed at the general public but does include some useful sections and opinions aimed more at the noise professional. There is a paid tutorial section for anyone wishing to learn more about noise, but the site also has a range of easy to read and informative articles.

http://noisenuisance.org/

World Health Organisation

The World Health Organisation has a large number of publications on environmental and occupational noise which are available for download, including reports on hearing loss, effects of noise on mental health, cardiovascular disease and childhood learning and development. It has suggested standards or criteria for noise, such as for environmental noise, annoyance and sleep disturbance in its publication "Community Noise 1999".

More recently the WHO have produced the Environmental Noise Guidelines for the European Region 2018. This examines the following sources of noise: road, rail, aircraft, wind turbines and leisure noise. This document examine the effects of these noise sources and suggests some guidelines which governments should consider in order to reduce the impacts of noise on health.

Many other health issues are covered, and noise topics may not always be easily found, but a large volume of authoritative research, guidance and information is available via their website.

http://www.who.int/en/

www.ingramcontent.com/pod-product-compliance
Lightning Source LLC
Chambersburg PA
CBHW040134240726
48664CB00002B/478